Walk In The Desert

Walk In The Desert

❖

Two true stories

By Helen MacKinnon

Writers Club Press
San Jose New York Lincoln Shanghai

Walk In The Desert
Two true stories

Writers Club Press
an imprint of iUniverse, Inc.

For information address:
iUniverse, Inc.
5220 S. 16th St., Suite 200
Lincoln, NE 68512
www.iuniverse.com

ISBN: 0-595-22407-5

Printed in the United States of America

To my husband, who has been my strength for more than half a century and to my children who have contributed so much of the material for this book.

Contents

VALLEY OF TEARS

PROLOGUE

When this traumatic episode happened in my life, painful as it was, I had a burning desire to hold onto the memories of it. For months I would wake in the night and literally re-live all of these events almost as if to burn them indelibly in my mind. I seemed to have an inner urge to write these things down, but then I would tell myself that I lived through something many before me had lived through and sadly I'm sure many after me will live through experiences equally as painful. This desire to write these things down must be my way of wanting to immortalize Ellen, I thought. Some of the most significant things such as "The Story of a Rose", I did jot down just for my own memories and I've found these original writings most helpful at this time.

About six or seven months after Ellen's death, my husband was requested to take a teacher's course on visitations to the sick, dying and elderly. Since his ministry of a Deacon Catholic Chaplin involved hospital and home visitations, he was a likely candidate to train others for this work. From this course the seeds of Hospice type of support would develop. He wanted to accept the offer to take the course but it would mean adding another 45 or 50 miles of driving twice a week to the 100 miles he already drove to and from work each day. This part was not appealing to him. For this reason, I volunteered to accompany him to the course to help with the driving. It was not my intention to actually participate in the course, however it turned out to be so interesting that I found myself totally involved. A few months later we were asked to participate in the teaching of two separate courses. We were able at this time to share some of our own experiences to clarify some of the teachings to the students. This seemed to bring that "inner urge to write things down", to the surface again, and so I followed my gut feelings. Years have passed since that time and whenever I say the prayer" Hail

Holy Queen" the same thought plagues my mind. I constantly remember saying this prayer as a child and as a young adult and thinking of the words "mourning and weeping in this valley of tears". I guess I was blessed with a happy childhood but I actually wondered what the words could possibly mean. "This Valley of Tears"—It was no valley of tears to me.

As an adult I've learned quite differently. Everywhere I look I see mourning and weeping and I'm well acquainted with it in my own life. Now the prayer means so much more to me.

Writing this has been both a joy and a therapy for me through the years, some serious, some funny. With all the stories, essays, dialogues and whatever else I've written, I always intended to pick up these pages I typed out so quickly so long ago, but when I tried, I'd find I was not emotionally up to it. Now some 16 years later, I have a peace that allows me to travel through that valley in memory.

I pray this story will answer the question Hannah Hurnard asks in her book <u>Winged Life</u>, "Will this book give news of the wonderful ways in which He teaches His people, and supports and strengthens them under testings and fiery trials?" (P.105)

To those whose lives will be touched by reading this, I want to say that this is my story, the way I remember it. If I left out things that others feel should also be remembered—so be it. If their memories of certain events differ slightly from the way I remember them—so be it. It is my thoughts, my memories, and my feelings, my "Valley Of Tears".

THE DECENT

March 8, 1979

"Will you accept a collect call from San Francisco, California?"

"Yes I will."

What is she doing still in California, she's supposed to be on her way back east.

"Ellen, what are you doing in California? I thought you'd be on your way back."

"Well mom, I got delayed, you see I'm calling from a hospital in San Francisco."

"Oh my God, I've been waiting for this call, you're going to tell me something awful—what is it?"

"I've got Leukemia."

I remembered back about six years. She came home from a prayer meeting at the Cenacle in Brighton and told me about this fellow, I'll call Alfred, who came up to her and asked if he could paint her picture. I figured he was using this to get to know her better. Why not? She was young, pretty and full of life. Alfred arrived a couple of days later and he was not what I expected. He was perhaps in his late twenties, lean with a full head of hair and a beard. His eyes were gentle. He drove an old car with "Jesus Loves You" painted in big letters on each side. He claimed he preached a sermon as he drove. A very unique fellow, he scouted all around he house looking for a place with the right lighting to do the painting. Ellen sat by his chosen window as he set up his easel and went to work.

We think of paintings as taking many hours of many sittings, but not Alfred's. Give him a canvas, paints and a few hours and he's captured an unreal likeness on canvas.

I went about my business doing my usual chores, but after a couple of hours I got nosey and went into the room where the artist was working.

"Is it alright to peek?"

"Sure, if you want to."

Of course I wanted to. I walked around the easel, for one split second I had a strange feeling of shock.

"Someday, you'll only have this painting to look at" a voice in my head seemed to say. I quickly brushed that awful feeling aside and remarked on the beauty of the likeness he was capturing in such rich colors. This guy was really gifted. Ellen was excited at my reaction. She hadn't seen the painted canvas at all. When I hung up the phone I sobbed and cried. I could see the framed portrait from where I sat. Ellen was going to die.

◆   ◆   ◆

My husband Bill was doing his visitations at the hospital. He would bring communion, counsel and pray with patients as part of his ministry as a Catholic Deacon. He has often come home and talked to me of the sorrow and sadness he shared with patients trying desperately to accept their own deaths. As I tearfully sat thinking of that fateful phone call, I remember thinking, "Now you must face it in your own home."

The two younger boys heard me sobbing and came from the downstairs family room where they were doing homework. I looked at them and in a flash, I thought of their youth and the awfulness of having to deal with tragedy at a young age. I guess I subconsciously prayed that the Lord would be near to sustain all of us.

"I might as well tell you now, you'll have to know anyway. Ellie has leukemia."

They stood stunned.

These are the two boys that Ellie and her sister Kathy, two years older, called "the minis."

The two little brothers that the two older sisters would bathe, get ready for bed and spoil to their heart's content. Kathy was married now with two children of her own, but Ellie had just completed her Master's Degree in Fine Arts and was excited about her career. She was still very family involved. Only two years before she was teaching at an Art Camp in Maine for the summer. She brought her two younger brothers for three glorious weeks where they stored up memories for a lifetime. Now those two boys stood staring at me as they tried to absorb the words I had spoken. Ellie has leukemia.

Sometime later, Bill came in from the hospital. He sensed immediately that things were not right. I, with tearful eyes, put my arms around his neck. We embraced as he asked, "what's wrong?"

I stood back just far enough to look into his eyes and said, "Ellie called from a hospital in California—she has leukemia."

The color drained from his face, and from his lips came "Jesus, Mary and Joseph." He stood silently, covering his face with his hands. After a moment I said, "She wants you to call her." He lowered his hands from his face and summoned the two boys to join us in a prayer before he could make that call.

Dennis our oldest boy teaches school in Alaska. He flew to California as he was closer than we were. Matt, her fiancé, flew from New York. Dennis kept us posted on exactly what was going on. Ellie's only hope was to have chemotherapy treatments. She wanted to come home and have them in Boston. We made arrangements with our doctor to bring her to a Boston hospital where she would be treated. The doctors would release her from the California hospital when they could control her pain long enough for the trip. On Sunday, Dennis helped get her on the plane along with Matt and the doctor, who gave her injections and pills for pain during the trip. Dennis then headed back to Alaska with plans to come home in the summer when Ellie would be in remission. We picked Ellie and Matt up at the airport. What a feeling to see her being pushed by Matt in a wheel chair. It was like some dream or fantasy that wasn't really happening.

I wrote that night in my journal.

March 11 Sunday:

We met Ellen and Matt at the airport and brought her to University Hospital. It was just three days ago that she found out that she had leukemia. She's in severe pain at times and the pain frightens her. She told me she thinks she's going to die at those times. She told me she'd never forget what I said to her on the phone. I didn't remember. She reminded me that I said, "I've been waiting for this call. You're going to tell me something awful, what is it?" She wanted to know what I meant, but I couldn't really explain that strange feeling I've had that we would loose her. Oh God, what strange ways do you use to prepare us to carry the burdens that we must bear? Be with Ellen to give her your strength and be with each member of our family. Bring good from this evil dread disease. Show your glory through it.

Now that decisions were made on the immediate problem we had another important decision to make. Mary our 20-year-old daughter had been born very prematurely and after seven weeks in isolation her progress was slow and many emotional problems surfaced. With a great deal of attention and therapy through the years she began to progress pretty well. Adolescence took its toll on her and when she was 16 she had a major nervous breakdown. This period of time is a whole other story, but briefly she had been in and out of hospitals for the past four years. At this time she was "in" the hospital. How do we tell her about Ellen? We called her doctor and he met with her therapists. They all determined that she should be told the truth, and so we had the added trauma of telling Mary of her beloved sister's situation and of not knowing how she would react. We consoled ourselves with the knowledge that the professionals were aware of the situation and ready to help her get through this. I remember her asking, "Is Ellen going to die?" It was hard to explain that we hoped not but that it could happen. She cried. We cried. It felt like things couldn't get worse for how could we stand it? Two of three daughters in two different hospitals. It seemed like some kind of nightmare. I would wake up and it would all be a bad dream. But no, I knew that was wishful thinking. We had to keep going. It was all too real. I felt like the energizer bunny, just going and going on batteries. By now, you the reader must realize that we are a large family. There were seven children. Dennis at that time was age 29, Kathy age 27, Ellen 25, Rod 23, Mary 20,Scott 16, and Donald 14. Rod was in Medical school at Tufts University. We deliberately choose not to put Ellen in New England Medical Center, which is affiliated with Tufts, fearing that Rod would get overly involved. However, as it turned out he would cross Boston every chance he could to be with Ellen and us. He happened to be studying leukemia at this time. Sometimes I wonder how many things in life are coincidences.

◆   ◆   ◆

On the way into the hospital the next morning I thought of the kind of person Ellen was. In many ways she was an idealist as I suppose are many who pursue the arts.

She stopped eating meat at about the age of 19. Her reason—with two thirds of the world going to bed hungry, if people ate less meat, less grain would be used to feed cattle and more would be available for the hungry nations. This was her "drop in the bucket" for humanity. She became very health conscious because she realized she had to obtain protein in other ways than from meat. Just the summer before she had told one of her cousins that she was the healthiest one in the family, and at that time I would have been inclined to agree with her. Her field of Art was Sculpture, so she was used to handling heavy materials. Everyone joked and kidded her for being so small yet so strong. Imagine the dynamics that had to take place when someone so young and healthy suddenly is faced with this diagnosis.

Shortly after our arrival at the hospital the doctor called a meeting with Ellen, parents, Matt, who was also an artist, and the nurses. He said, "There is no cure for leukemia, but we can try for remission." I heard these words like a death sentence and couldn't believe the questions Ellen was asking the doctor. Things like, "Will the chemotherapy make me sterile?" She talked about marrying and going to New York to continue her Artwork, after her remission. She said she'd heard that you don't even feel sick when you're in remission. From her point of view she would get this remission and life would go on.

I was very tired that night and only wrote a few lines.

March 12 Monday

A very difficult day. The doctor met with all of us and pulled no punches. There is no cure for Ellie's leukemia, acute myelogenous. We will try for remission beginning tomorrow. Her pain was intense. It was heart breaking.

The chemotherapy kills good blood cells as well as bad. For this reason the doctor decided that Ellen would have reverse precaution. This meant that before entering her room everyone, staff included, would have to put on gowns, masks, headgear and gloves. This precaution was used to protect Ellen from any germs that might be brought in, as she would have less and less natural immunity; as the chemotherapy increased. No plants or flowers would be allowed in her room either. The last time she saw our faces in many weeks other than our eyes was that Tuesday morning.

Now emotions were becoming more intense. On looking back I realize that we the parents, and Ellen the patient, were very often at different places. I found myself getting angry that Matt seemed to always be there and I could never have Ellen to myself. I could never admit that to anyone but still it hurt. By Friday Bill and I felt we needed to talk to someone objectively. We made an appointment with Father Hughes at the Seminary. He was able to make us realize that we had to just be there to support her and allow her to make all decisions even though we may sometimes feel left out. It was hard to have your heart breaking and try to hide it. That night I wrote the following in my journal.

March 16 Friday

We went to the hospital as usual doing our best to keep our feelings in check. We left to keep an appointment with Father Hughes at the Seminary and were able to express to him our heartaches and feelings.

Thank you Lord for giving us Father Hughes to turn to. Your presence can be felt and heard through him. Now you have directed us as to our role in this situation, and although it is not an easy one we will try to follow it trusting in your grace to carry us through.

On Sunday she had friends arrive and I could feel the anger welling up in me. I tried not to show it.

March 18 Sunday

Ellen had too darn much company. After she requested that only our immediate family come in during the chemotherapy, still plenty of her friends showed up—too many.

March 19 Monday

Had blood drawn for platelet match. Everyone in the family will have this done and the best matches will be used when she needs them. All ten days of the chemotherapy were horrible, with just about every emotion imaginable involved. Everyone tried so hard to "do something," but after all is said and done, prayer was the only thing we could do.

On Thursday, March 22, I wrote the last entry I was to put in my journal for many months. It reads: Our resistance is getting pretty low. Father Hughes called and this was a great lift. He is constantly praying about this. Matt is going to New York for the weekend. Mary was given a pass to go to see Ellen by herself, a good step or her. Rod is studying Leukemia in Med School. He's always in the hospital. It is very difficult for him. To-morrow is the bone marrow. Oh Lord, it is in your hands.

The next morning we had breakfast and were gathering things to take, when the phone rang. It was Ellen and she was very excited. "Mom", she said, "we had a strange little hale storm this morning and it coincided with the very time the needle was put in for the bone marrow. The sun came out afterwards as the needle was being extracted. It's a sign." The results wouldn't be known until later in the day, but she was feeling very optimistic.

I thought about the hale storm and the sun and marveled that she could see the hand of God at this sorrowful time. The laughter and happiness in her voice on the phone made me think of the gift of laughter. It truly is a gift when we can laugh even when we are in the depths of sadness. I began to think of the moments of laughter we had had, even in these past two weeks. One thing really stood out in my mind, as I laughed until nearly on the brink of tears. The chemotherapy can have many side effects. Very common are loss of hair and nausea and vomiting. Some of the nurses "dropped the hint" that smoking marijuana relieved the nauseous feeling. But since it was not yet used as a medicinal drug it could not be legally administered. They indicated that if it were brought in from outside the hospital they most likely wouldn't notice it. Matt, Bill, Ellen and I sat around in the room discussing how we could get some marijuana. Of course one thing led to another and we did a lot of joking about Dad trying to get it and what if the Deacon got picked up for possession of marijuana! Matt was able to get the drug, we never asked how, and Ellen would smoke it when she felt nauseous. We laughed a lot about STRAIGHTS like ourselves being in on such a ploy. Kathy's husband George bought a beautiful, fancy water cooler so that the marijuana would be cool on Ellen's throat. One day right in the midst of this "treatment" a Newscast came on television. It said that the legislature was considering legalizing marijuana for medicinal purposes. We all cheered in unison right in that hospital room.

As Ellie had been going through the chemotherapy she had been warned that loss of hair was one of the side effects. Friends had brought her funny hats and we brought in a wig. She joked about these things but never put them on. She just had them placed around the room like decorations. Each day she or someone else would comment that she still had her hair, but apparently it was beginning to thin out with pieces coming out as it was brushed. One morning when we arrived, she had a scarf on her head, She said that rather than watch it come out a little at a time, and she had one of the nurses shave it off. We were surprised but thought perhaps it was easier that way. At this point she was able to joke about her baldhead. She asked if I would buy her a black cotton scarf, as she always preferred the natural materials rather than the synthetics. She was like her Dad in that respect. The cotton scarf I brought in was the one she kept on her head thereafter.

On Scott's first visit after the hair was gone, we were all sitting, gowned and masked, talking to each other. Ellen was having one of her good moments and conversed fluently with us. A couple of times she said to Scott, "Do you want to see my bald head?" He either didn't hear or pretended he didn't. But she was persistent and repeated it to him very directly. It was obvious to Matt, Bill and I that she wanted him to look. Matt was standing beside the bed but back far enough that Ellen couldn't see his face. He bowed his head to Scott as if to say answer yes. So Scott said, "Yea O.K." I was feeling apprehensive but tried not to show it. Ellen reached with her one free hand (the other had a needle attached) and took the scarf off. Much to my delight Scott handled himself beautifully. He smiled at Ellie and said, "You and Telly Savellis." We all were able to laugh together and what might have been a miserable incident turned out fine, thanks to laughter. I've often thought of that incident and asked myself why she did that. I suppose in her own way she was saying, "love me as I am." Or perhaps she was thinking that we had to see to really believe what she was going through. Whatever her reason, his answer was certainly guided by a higher power.

The results of the bone marrow came back later in the day. The leukemia cells were still there. Ellen sobbing and crying, "I'm only 25 I don't want to die." We hugged and kissed and tried to console each other. There was Ellie with her baldhead and tears, Matt, Dad and myself in tears. For the first time I felt a bond with Matt because of

Ellen's love for him. We could only love each other as human beings. We were helpless except for love. It was heartbreaking. When all the tears were shed, plans to start a second chemo began.

THE VALLEY

A new phase begins. While sorrow and painfulness seemed to deepen, healing seemed to be taking place too. Love truly abounded and priorities seemed to be falling into the right places. Ellen now lost her enthusiasm for casual friends. It was important that her times of being well enough to converse and enjoy people be reserved for those closest to her.

The second chemotherapy began and the realization that the remission had less of a chance than before had hit all of us. Paula, the psychologist, visited often during this time. The nurses were also helpful psychologically as well as physically. Many of them had become Ellen's friends and many were very near her own age. The one thing that really disturbed Bill and me was that we didn't think Ellen was getting enough spiritual support. Psychological help is certainly necessary, but there is such strength in spiritual support. We were sure that our own strength would have been exhausted by now, were it not for our own prayer life and the many prayers of friends. We wanted Ellen to have this kind of support too. Father Hughes had told us that he would contact a sister that he knew who did this type of counseling at University Hospital, but no sister ever came.

Now the hospital was the only place we wanted to be, but because we still had a house to run and the two boys were going to high school, one a freshman, the other a junior, we had to spend some time at home. We would leave the hospital at nine or ten at night. Sleep, even with medication, was fitful and the phone was always beside the bed. Many of my nights were spent sitting in the living room praying and looking at the beautiful portrait. Everywhere I looked in the house are loving signs of Ellen. For years now our gifts from her were created objects, fruits of her artistry. I could look in the fireplace and see a grate she had made, turn my eyes slightly to the left to see a lovely white plaster form, an art piece. On the coffee table is one of my favorites, an anniversary gift. She called it her hen ladies. It consists of two figures, a combination of people and hens in bronze, standing on a thick aluminum base. There are many more gifts; perhaps the most sentimental being a framed pressed rose which covers diagonally half the area in the frame. The other half is plain white. When she gave it to me on Mother's Day, less than a year before, she explained that it was symbolic of our relationship. "The part of the frame filled with the rose represents the things that we know about each other and the plain white area is symbolic of the things we don't know about one another. The white is an envelope and I've written a note to you in it." I kissed her and told her how beautiful it was. I knew she realized that no matter how well people know one another, there is always that very private part known only to our selves. I never opened the envelope up to that time. Bill and I would rise early in the mornings and call the hospital immediately. Often we would talk to Ellen and if she were doing fairly well she might ask that we bring a little ice cream or some other thing that she wanted. Any errands such as getting groceries for the house were done as early as possible so that we could get back to that place where our hearts always remained.

◆   ◆   ◆

Bill and I spent much time together in silence, each engrossed in our own thoughts. During our trips back and forth to the hospital we often played a tape of modern day hymns. Bill had heard these songs at Kathy and George's house and liked them, so George made copies. He is thoughtful that way. We seemed to gain strength from the words of the songs. Bill thought Ellen might find the same solace from these songs so he copied the tape for her. When he gave it to her she said, "Oh Dad, you're going to play hymns. Don't make me feel like I'm dying." He just left the tape on the table in her room saying she might enjoy listening to it another time. I don't think she listened to it very much. There were other times though that we knew she did think about dying. Like the day I was in the room with her and she looked at me and said, "I guess it's true Ma, you get the ticket when you get to the train." She was referring to the book The <u>Hiding Place</u> by Corrie Ten Boom. This book about a family that hid Jews in Germany during World War II had a very touching section in it where Corrie asks her father not to die. He answers her with great wisdom.

"Corrie, when you and I go to Amsterdam—when do I give you your ticket?"

"Why, just before we get on the train."

"Exactly. And our wise Father in heaven knows when we're going to need things too. Don't run out ahead of him Corrie. When the time comes that some of us will have to die, you will look into your heart and find the strength you need—just in time."

I knew then that she felt the necessary grace to go through this nightmare. Something I'm sure she never would have felt herself capable of bearing a few months before. Ellen had begun her spiritual journey inward. The things of this world that are so fleeting, yet so highly valued, began to have less relevance to her. Her own inner affairs took precedence and she wanted to organize those things and prepare for death. Her feelings were fluctuating between a determination to live and the fact that she very possibly would die.

Another time when we were together she asked what I thought of the idea that trials in our lives prepare us for even greater crosses. I said that I thought it was true that each trial built us in strength for future trials. Her answer, "Well God sure started me out with a biggy."

Only with that answer did I realize how selfish my thinking was. Here I was thinking of the trials and tribulations in my own life building me up for the great one I was now facing and I totally neglected to think of what Ellen was herself facing. How often I've thought about that and asked God's forgiveness. I know that for the rest of my life I must try not to make that mistake again. How weak we are! So engrossed in our own feelings that we tend to forget the sufferings of others.

♦   ♦   ♦

Word was spreading about Ellen's illness. Friends and relatives were trying to be as supportive as possible. Cards were pouring into the hospital. Many, many prayers were being said. Our Deacon friend Phil wrote:

> "Continued prayers to Saint Therese who knows all about you and with whom you share a special place, through her intercession, in the heart of Jesus, for you too are a little one."

Heaven was being stormed in Ellen's behalf and the power of those prayers could truly be felt, even though physically it was straight down hill. Not one thing that was tried seemed to work. Her veins on both arms were so dissipated that the intravenous needle had to be put in her neck. Here was the little girl who dreaded to even go to the dentist to have her teeth cleaned, now bearing up under all these medical procedures. How do I explain the presence of God under such conditions, and yet we knew and felt his peace.

♦   ♦   ♦

Bill and I went looking for the Sister and we found her. It seemed she knew of this case. Father Hughes had spoken with another older nun, and when the message reached Sister Eleanor she thought that the patient's parents wanted the local priest to come into the hospital and anoint her. She knew that would be a traumatic thing to do to a young girl. When she realized that we just wanted her to become Ellen's friend, to bring God in herself to Ellen, she started that day to visit with her.

Our days in the hospital were lengthening. It was becoming more difficult each night to leave. What a blessing to come home and find that friends from town and church were sending suppers in for the boys. The time spent shopping and cooking could now be spent in the hospital.

We prayed as we looked for signs. My sister sent me a plant, a Christmas cactus that she had since she lost a son nine years before and it had never bloomed until now. She split the plant and sent me the half with the one blossom on it.

Plants and flowers also came to the hospital for Ellen but they could not be brought into her room. Dennis called her several times from Alaska and the hope for the summer meeting continued, at least on the surface.

Holy week was fast approaching and the second chemotherapy was coming to an end. We waited with apprehension for the bone marrow results.

We knew the answer before we were told.

We saw the psychologist in the corridor. Sister was there too. They each visited her after the doctor gave her the news. We even saw and heard a nurse, with tears in her eyes, tell another nurse that Ellie was going to die. When we went into her room, she was just turned into herself.—Silence—Depression.

◆   ◆   ◆

Not only had the chemotherapy failed again but also now there was the complication of an infection. "Infection of unknown origin" as it was medically written up.

> "How long, 0 Lord will you utterly forget me?
> How long will you hide your face from me?
> How long shall I harbor sorrow in my soul,
> Grief in my heart day after day?
> Look, answer me, 0 Lord, my God."   (Ps. 13, 1–4)

All day Saturday, the day before Palm Sunday, the doctors and staff worked feverishly to try to beat the infection. Antibiotics were not sufficient and Ellen would periodically run extremely high temperatures.

The doctor told us of a new machine the hospital had just recently acquired which, among other things, could remove blood from the donor and separate certain white cells, before returning the remaining blood back into the system. It was, at the time, the only machine of it's kind in the Boston area. Bill, Scott and Rod were chosen as the closest matches to Ellen's blood so their white cells would be used to combat the infection.

Here Lord is my miracle, I thought. The only machine of it's kind in the area. Even in the depths of despair, hope continues to spring eternal. There even seemed to be a kind of joy in this opportunity. Whether or not we were the chosen one we all seemed to have the feeling we were really "doing" something. Ellen would even manage little jokes with us, like: "Let's see how good your cells are?"

Oh Lord, was this another chance?

It was necessary that Matt leave periodically for a couple of days. No one could survive such circumstances without breaking away once in awhile. Bill would spend the night with Ellen.

It was about ten P.M. and I was preparing to leave the hospital. Usually there was someone with me when I drove home at night, but this night I would make the trip alone. Just before I was to leave the hospital, an unusual experience took place. Ellen's bed was raised to a half sitting position and she had fallen asleep. Bill was sitting on one side of the bed and I on the other. He was giving me last minute instructions about locking the car doors etc., when suddenly Ellen woke, leaned forward and said, "Shh, I'm listening to the voices." At that Bill and I were silent and stared in shock at one another and at her. She continued, "They're saying, many are called but few are chosen." She kept staring into space and we waited for more, but there was no more. After only brief moments she closed her eyes and lay back, asleep again. Bill and I looked at each other in wonder. I said good-night to him, kissed her too and left the hospital. All the way home I seemed to feel a spiritual high. It wasn't until later that I found out that my "high" was practically a valley compared with the awesome night Bill had spent.

◆   ◆   ◆

BILL'S STORY AS TOLD TO ME

"Many are called but few are chosen." Words we've heard so many times and perhaps dismissed them because they're so difficult to understand. There was a cot in the room but I decided not to use it because I didn't want to fall asleep in case Ellen woke, so I sat on a straight back chair. I began to meditate on those words. I thought of God's love and how he loves each of us exactly as we are. As I meditated on His love for man, I realized what a bind God is in. He has promised to love us no matter what, and He cannot go back on His word. We don't have to love Him, but He has to love us. "Many are called," but I thought, we are all called. Yes, God is calling and loving all of us, and here we are, most of us paying no attention to Him. Like a revelation, the light dawned. "Few are chosen"—of course—how few recognize that love and hear that call. How few turn around and look back to respond to that love. Few choose to love God.

Over and over this whole concept ran through my brain and I felt such love for God I think I was in ecstasy. I don't know how much time passed, but I was drawn back to reality when I saw Ellen open her eyes. I had to share my meditation with her. When I talked to her about God's love for us, a sweet smile crossed her lips and she closed her eyes again. I never quite knew whether that smile meant, "Thank you for telling me Dad" or "Now you know Dad." Either way, it was the most precious and spiritual moment of my life.

Later that same night her temperature rose up so high that she had to be packed in ice. Her crying and anguish were heart breaking. I must have soaked fifteen masks with tears. Yet in the depths of sorrow there was the presence of God. That night was one of deepest sorrow and tremendous joy simultaneously."

The next morning we attended Mass in the hospital chapel. It was Palm Sunday. Palm Sunday—Holy Week—Passion Week.

There is tremendous meditation in just thinking of that week. It seems that nothing is coincidence. Surely the Lord has a message for us in allowing such enormous sorrow and suffering. How much greater that message becomes when it falls on the very week that we remember the sorrows and sufferings of Jesus.

Sister Eleanor continued to visit each day. She and Ellen had established a beautiful relationship.

The fever was frightening. Each time it shot up, the question of life itself was at stake. The process of the white cells from Bill, Rod and Scott had begun. It would be awhile before we knew if it would work. My miracle—of course it would work.

I wanted very much to be the one to spend this night alone with Ellen. After much insistence to Bill that I really wanted to do this, he consented to go home that night and let me stay. Rod kept stalling around and I could tell that he just wasn't going to leave. That old feeling of wanting Ellen to myself for a while was coming back again and I found myself having trouble not acting resentful. I began to wonder if Rod and his Dad had contrived this so that I would not be alone there. There seemed to be no way to make them understand. Yet as I sat in the room with Ellen sleeping (Rod was in the hospital, but not in the room) I knew it was wrong of me to be so possessive, but I just couldn't help it. I prayed.

> Hasten to answer me, 0 Lord,
> For my spirit fails me.
> Hide not your face from me
> Lest I become like those who
> Go down into the pit.   Ps.142, 7

Matt came back during the night. That night was not to be mine alone. Ellen opened her eyes and I forced myself to smile and say, "See whose here Ellie!"

The smile that came on her lips convicted me of my own selfishness.

Thank you Lord for loving me even in my misery. When moments like this let me see myself as I really am, I marvel that you, so perfect, continue to love each of us who can never be worthy of that perfect love.

> 0 Lord you have probed me and you know me;
> You know when I sit and when I stand;
> You understand my thoughts from afar.
> My journeys and my rest you scrutinize,
> With all my ways you are familiar.
> Even before a word is on my tongue,
> Behold, 0 Lord, you know the whole of it.
> Behind me and before, you hem me in
> And rest your head upon me.
> Such knowledge is too wonderful for me,
> Too lofty for me to attain.   Ps. 13 9, 1–6

◆   ◆   ◆

This was truly a "holy week." Every treatment of blood cells, platelets, whole blood, everything that was done, seemed to be followed by high temperatures, ice packs, pain and suffering—sheer agony.

"It looks like I might not even make it to my birthday", were her words to me at one point. My answer could only be silence. Her birthday was a month away.

Prayers were rising like incense to heaven. Everyone we knew and so many we didn't know were praying. Friends and relatives called prayer lines and assisted at Masses. The Benedictines at Glastonbury Abbey, especially our dear friend Father Roger, offered their prayer and support. Heaven was being stormed in Ellen's behalf. What better week in all the year for prayer than Holy Week! All of us were truly living holy week with Christ, but most important, Ellen was living and joining the agonies of Jesus. One might ask: "What about these prayers? Why weren't they answered?" I knew even then, as I know now that they have been and still are being answered. Answered prayer is not always the miracle of a physical healing. Prayers bring about a healing that continues to go on. A spiritual healing far greater than any physical healing could ever be. To be able to accept without reservations, to truly turn everything over to God as Jesus did in the garden when He said to His Father, "take this cup from me" and then added, "not my will, but thine be done." This is healing. This is the healing all of us watched take place in Ellen during Holy Week. This is the healing that is slowly, ever so slowly, taking place in me.

By Good Friday she was so weak and sick that at one point I whispered in her ear, "It's Good Friday Ellie, offer your sufferings up with Jesus." She answered, "I am."

I knew we were both remembering about six years before, when we had gone together to hear Bishop Sheen speak at Hynes Auditorium in Boston on Good Friday. He spoke of the wasted sufferings in hospitals because they were not offered up with the sufferings of Jesus.

That day she asked for Father Hughes to come to her.

◆   ◆   ◆

The next day, Holy Saturday, we were in her room waiting for Father Hughes to arrive. As I said before, Ellen had some good moments mixed with the bad. On this particular day she didn't even seem rational when she talked. I wondered how much of what we said was even understood by her. When the priest arrived I was upset for fear that she may not be able to talk to him or might not even realize that he was there. Bill, unlike me, was sure everything would be all right. But as usual, I had to get myself into the act. Lord will I never learn? I proceeded to begin explaining to father as he was "gowning up," that she had been irrational and may not be able to communicate with him. He was calm as always and didn't seem the least concerned about that. He entered her room and spent quite a bit of time alone with her. When the door opened he informed us that they had had a good conversation and now she would like us to come into the room while she received the sacrament of the sick. Sister Eleanor, Matt, Bill and I all joined Ellen in prayer as Father administered the sacrament. As we talked later we realized she had been totally conscious and rational the whole time Father Hughes was with her. She even thanked us for having met him through us.

I repeat, "Lord, will I never learn?"

My sister sent a whole Easter dinner and it was at the house Saturday night when we arrived home. Scott would be going on the machine for the white blood cells Easter morning, so we just brought the food and the boys with us and headed for the hospital. We attended Mass in the hospital chapel and then Bill brought Scott to the blood bank area before going up to the floor Ellie was on. The doctor was with her so we waited. When he left her room he told us that she requested that he send Sister Eleanor and us into her room. We all gathered around her bed. With tears in her eyes she announced that since she would soon die, she wanted no more treatment other than to be kept comfortable. She would like the "reverse precaution" taken off so she could see the ones she loved. She would like flowers in her room and only Matt, the family and Sister Eleanor visiting. She asked Sister Eleanor if she would be with her when she died.

The doctor was waiting to speak with us when we went outside to take off our gowns etc. He told us how he had explained to Ellen that the white cells were just not enough to fight the infection. Medically there was no hope. I asked if she had made the right decision. "I think she made the best decision" was his answer. Scott was taken off the machine. For the first time in five weeks Ellen could look at our faces. Both joy and sorrow prevailed.

Acceptance took place on Resurrection Day.

Easter Sunday took on a new meaning for us in more ways than one. Throughout the day our daughter called for little meetings. She was always "chairman of the board" at these meetings and in a gentle loving way she made her wishes known to us.

She decided on a simple wake with her body in a closed "PINE BOX." She would like to be cremated rather than take up Real Estate that the living could use. Would we request that people who wanted to send flowers instead donate money to the Leukemia fund? The white roses she had requested from her brother Dennis should be put into the coffin with her as a symbol of her brother's presence who was physically so far away. They had made this decision by telephone the night before. Would she have to wear a dress? She'd rather just be in her jeans that she wore while doing her artwork. I said I didn't really think it mattered, since no one would see her anyway. In that case she'd like her cowboy boots put on her too.

WHAT AN UNBELIEVABLE CONVERSATION! She hadn't mentioned the ashes and I remember thinking that I hoped she wouldn't. I wanted us to at least keep the ashes. Bill was more straightforward than I. He came right out and asked if he could have her ashes.

Oh! She hadn't thought of that.—(I could have killed him).

"What will you do with them?" she asked in a kind of sarcastic tone.

"I'll put them on the mantel, he answered in the same tone. "Aren't you afraid they'll spill on the rug?"

"If they do I can vacuum them up."

"Yes, you can have them."

"Thank you Ellie, they'll be buried with Mom and me."

We consented to all her wishes and she said, "You can decide anything else." I didn't say it, but I thought—"what else?"

THE STORY OF A ROSE

When I was young I had a great devotion to Saint Therese of the child Jesus, more commonly known as "The Little Flower."

Before her death at the age of 24, she said she would spend her eternity doing good on earth and she would let fall a shower of roses. Roses have since been symbolic of Saint Therese. I grew up in a city parish where each year there was a novena to Saint Therese and on the ninth day of the novena there was a large procession. The high light of this procession was a girl dressed as Saint Therese. One girl from the high school senior class was chosen for this honor. Each year all through school I made this novena, so you can imagine my delight when as a senior I was chosen to be saint Therese in this procession. As the years went by my devotion to Saint Therese would wane. Parish novenas became a thing of the past, but I always have had that marvelous memory which would periodically bring me back to praying to her to intercede to God for me.

About seven or eight years before this time, I met a friend of Bill's who has one of the greatest devotions to this powerful saint that I had ever seen. I remember commenting on the fact that Saint Therese seems to keep popping up in my life and when she does I feel led to pray to her.

She came back very strongly to my mind and thoughts as I watched Ellen so sick but still so beautiful. I would find myself thinking that Saint Therese must have looked young and lovely as Ellen, but also weak and ill. They were close to the same age too, Ellen only one year older. I felt very compelled to call upon this saint in Ellen's behalf. I started praying to her and one day while talking to one of my sisters about prayer, I told her of my inner urge to invoke the help of Saint Therese. Much to my surprise she told me that for many years she had a first class relic of this saint and that I could have it to bring to Ellen. Now I was sure that Saint Therese wanted to be part of our lives at this time.

I brought the relic to the hospital and told Ellen of our prayers so that she could join us in praying to Saint Therese too if she so desired. A short time later Ellen received a beautiful note from our friend Phil. He too was praying to Saint Therese. Later another note telling her that he continued to pray. It was only a few days before Easter and we knew that the Lord was calling Ellen home at this young age, as He called Saint Therese at a young age. A third note came from Phil and in it he said the following:

> "A novena to the Little Flower of Jesus for you. It is but a few days until a great liturgical feast in church, a feast of astounding promise and incomprehensible love! When on this forthcoming Easter day the first streaks of dawn break in the skies of Boston, Cohasset, Hingham, wherever—may the gentle peace of Him who is yet the conquering lover of people every where be in and about you and all close to you, both at this moment and always!"

When Ellen gave the note to Bill to read, he remembered what Phil would always say when he was making a novena for anyone. Bill said the words for him to Ellen, "Look for the rose." He then explained to Ellen that Phil claimed that a rose would somehow come into the life of the one being prayed for. In her usual spunky fashion she said, "Now Dad, don't go sending me a rose."

"Come on Ellie, you know I wouldn't do that." Her eyes sparkled and her lips smiled at his reply. We all knew that no flowers were allowed in her room anyway.

On Easter Sunday morning the doctor talked with Ellen explaining the hopelessness of all the efforts being made for her life. Everything had failed.

This was the first time she was able to accept her own death. On looking back, I realize that while we were all steeped in sorrow, there were also definite signs of the resurrection. Her decision was that all the reverse precaution, which required everyone who entered her room to put on gowns, gloves, masks etc., be removed. We could now enter in our regular clothes and she could for the first time in many weeks, look at our faces. Flowers could now be brought into her room too.

Our son Rod told us that he received a telephone call from our older son in Alaska. It seemed that Dennis had been talking to Ellen by phone the day before, which was Easter. She had requested that he send her white roses since he was unable to be with her himself. He had tried frantically and was unable to get white roses sent to her. He asked Rod if he would buy them and bring them to Ellen. When Rod tried to get the roses, he discovered that Boston was celebrating Patriot's Day, and everyplace that sold roses was closed, including the big flower exchange. The white roses would have to wait until Tuesday.

Bill and I were sitting in the large vestibule of the hospital corridor where we spent much of our time when we were not in Ellen's room. Suddenly Bill touched me and said, "LOOK." We saw a young friend who knew and loved Ellen since back in high school days, walking toward her room. This boy had a sister who was retarded but educable. Many times through the years he and Ellen would take the girl out for a day of fun. Ellen loved her. There was Jeannie, walking beside her brother and carrying one red rose. It had been purchased with the money Jeannie had earned herself.

Yes, "though I walk through the valley of the shadow of death I will fear no evil, for He is with me.

His rod and His staff, (and His saints) they comfort me."

Some of the scars and hurts we bury deep within us have a way of surfacing when the clock of time is running out. This is the time for resolving all hurts and airing all feelings freely. Sad as it is, it also has a certain beauty, an honesty that we often neglect in ordinary life.

Now there was no time for pretense. Thank God, truth prevailed. All the little hurts had to be laid out and resolved, but one conversation Ellie had with her father is unforgettable for him. It started with something small. She remembered being blamed and sent to her room for some childish infraction when she was a little girl. She didn't even remember the reason; only that she was unjustly punished. "You made me stay in my room and I didn't do it Dad. Kathy did it," she said with the old original hurt telling in her voice. "Can you forgive me Ellen?" her father responded. Then came, "I forgive you Dad, but when I came home from Delaware with my Master in Fine Arts degree and I showed you my portfolio—the results of <u>seven</u> years of my work and study in Art—you gave it ten minutes then closed the book to help Scott with a high school paper on Bill Kennedy."

My heart wrenched, as it does even now and every time I think of that conversation. I looked at Bill and the tears filled his eyes as he repeated with great emotion, "Ellen, can you forgive me?" "I forgive you Dad," she said gently as if she was relieved at the unburdening of this hurt she had carried for the past year.

I well remember the day she referred to. Strangely, up until that moment it had been a happy, fun like memory. We had finished supper and were sitting around the table talking and drinking tea. During the conversation Ellen said something about having brought her portfolio home with her. Bill said he'd like to see it. "Would you really like to see it?" she asked. On hindsight now I realize that her art had progressed beyond our understanding and she apparently had stopped expecting affirmation from us in that area. "Yes of course I would," he answered. She happily went to get the portfolio and brought it back to the table.

Bill began looking at the book of her work. After a short time passed, Scott came up from the playroom where he was doing homework and asked some question about Bill F. Kennedy. Bill looked up from Ellen's book and started talking to Scott about the paper he was writing. Of course Kennedy was a more familiar subject than things like "Depth Perception II in Art," so it was easy to slip from one subject to the other. As we started kidding Scott about some of his sentence structures and his repetition of the words "manifest destiny," Bill unconsciously closed the book in front of him and continued helping Scott. No one noticed Ellen take the book away or the hurt she must have been enduring. Not until this moment in the hospital room did we truly understand.

Dear Lord, how many times do we unconsciously hurt others, even those we love most in this world? "CAN YOU FORGIVE ME?"

Tears constantly flowed from Ellen's beautiful eyes. She claimed she must have an eye infection in them, but we knew it was the difficulty of saying good-bye. The nurse would periodically come in and put drops in her eyes and that kind of made it all right for tears to keep falling.

"I wonder what it's like to die?" she said.

Being the type of person that I am, I thought that question required an answer. But who can answer that! The feeble little thought that came into my mind was all I had to offer.

"I remember making a mission when I was a young girl Ellie. The priest was speaking on death. He told the story of a little boy who asked his father what it was like to die. His father answered him something like this, "You know Tommy, when you fall asleep in the living room and I carry you into your bed, you wake in the morning in your own bed. Well I believe that when we die, we close our eyes to this world and Our Father in heaven carries us to our own bed and we wake up at home in heaven.""

It wasn't much, but I suppose it was as good an answer as can be given at such a time.

Something was bothering me that I very much wanted to say and yet I wondered if it would be inappropriate. Somehow, when the moment seemed right, I just came out with the words. Looking into her eyes and very close to her, I finally said, "Ellie, when you meet the Lord, will you ask Him about Mary?" Notice I did not ask the lord or her to <u>do</u> anything, just to ask about. I simply wanted to understand. Her reply will always be one of the most precious moments of my life. It is not only precious to me, but it gave me the knowledge that my question was not in poor taste or inappropriate. She answered in her usual spirited way. "Oh Ma! You even have a job for me to do up there."

Sweet Ellen, I loved your answer then and I love it every time I think of it. Tears fall on my cheeks even as I write this and remember. I smiled and shook my head, "Yes".

Tuesday, April 17

The room was filled with the fragrance of roses. Two dozen white roses from Denny. Rod and his fiancée Alice brought red roses, and of course the special rose from Jeannie. During Ellen's lucid moments life still had a certain beauty to it. She talked of many things, about the Chinese New Year in California, and many different places she went to and things she did that gave her pleasant memories.

Kathy brought ice cream from Kimballs, a favorite ice cream place since they were little girls. Ellie challenged all of us to take her there. Matt said, "You know you're too sick to go out for ice cream". "I think you're all a bunch of stiffs", was her reply. Laughter again filled the room.

All the while, tears of joy and sorrow would trickle from her eyes as we shared that last special gift of each other's love.

◆   ◆   ◆

I don't remember much about Wednesday. For a very long time I could remember nothing about it. I couldn't understand why that day seemed to just blank out in my mind.

One day when I was talking to Kathy, I told her how I couldn't remember anything about the day before Ellen died. She reminded me of the only significant thing that happened that day.

Ellen was extremely weak and heavily medicated. The psychologist seemed to feel that she perhaps could not let go of life and suggested that we each in turn go in and say good-bye to her. We were to let her know in our own way that it was all right for her to leave us. I know I took my turn but do not know exactly what I said. All I know is that when I was reminded of that day, I realized why I had forgotten it. Apparently it was much too painful to remember and God in His mercy granted me the ability to forget.

◆   ◆   ◆

Early the next morning, about five o'clock, Bill called the hospital. She was just as we had left her the night before, heavily medicated and unresponsive. We began to slowly start another day. A short time later the phone rang. Ellen's vital signs began to fall. We hurried to get to the hospital. Fervently we prayed all the way that we might have one more opportunity to see her alive. After parking the car, we raced into the hospital and on to the elevator. From the elevator we ran down the corridor and into her room. Matt and Sister Eleanor were already there. Ellen laid peacefully, eyes closed, breathing heavily. She could not communicate but somehow I felt she knew we were there. Everything was just as she had requested. Her breathing became more and more spaced and slowly it just stopped. I remember clearly what my thoughts were at that moment. There we were looking at this body we so loved in life. I felt her presence, as if she were in the room watching this whole scene. I looked around the room almost expecting to see her, but she was no longer a part of the world we know. She had slipped from life, and was now born to eternal life.

LIFE and DEATH—WHAT MYSTERY

I remember the day she was born. Unlike some of my other children, her birth was quite peaceful. It was a Holy Day, Ascension Thursday. When I began my labor I thought it would be nice to have this baby enter the world on the holy day. It was about ten at night when Bill brought me to the hospital. At about eleven o'clock one of the nurses checked my progress and told me I had a way to go. I told her I planned on having the baby before midnight because this was a holy day. "You'll never make it" was her reply.

"Yes I will", said I.

Sure enough, Ellen made her entrance at eleven forty five, fifteen minutes to spare.

Something always seemed special about that. Born on Thursday, died on Thursday. Life and death—what mystery.

MOURNING and WEEPING

I t was over.

Or was it just beginning?

Rod arrived at the hospital just a few minutes later. "Were you both with her?" he asked.

"Yes."

"I'm glad."

As we walked through the hospital corridor he said something that I would later recall with much greater meaning. "If only she could come back—just once—and tell us that everything is alright." I guess that's the true pain of death. It's so final.

◆　　◆　　◆

"You can decide everything else," she had said. "What else?" I had thought.

But yes, there was something else. The Funeral Mass. She hadn't made any special requests concerning the Mass. This one small but important event would be our decision.

Once again came that feeling to <u>do</u> something. Now at least we could do something about the Mass.

Bill chose all the readings. I chose the hymns. It was not to be sad and somber. It should be as joyful as possible. After all, even though her life was short, hadn't she been able to convey some happiness to all of us right up to the end? A somber Funeral Mass just wouldn't be fitting.

◆   ◆   ◆

The wake was exactly as she had requested. I'm sure it was rather shocking to those who attended; it departed so strongly from a conventional wake. To both Bill and I and to many others it was very beautiful in it's simplicity. A rosary of roses which one of my sisters sent as a symbol of the Saint Therese experience, decorated the closed pine box.

On Saturday morning we entered a crowded church for the funeral. We wanted the Mass to be special, but we never could have dreamed it would be this special. The whole church had an aura of holiness. The altar was crowded with priests and deacons, a tribute to Bill whose friends had taken the time to come and celebrate the Holy Sacrifice of the Mass for Ellen.

0 Lord, this was the greatest blessing you could have given us.

One rose, placed by Matt, lay on top of the draped coffin. As it was brought down the aisle, the song we listened to so often in the car while driving to the hospital was beautifully sung.

Refrain: BE NOT AFRAID. I GO BEFORE YOU ALWAYS. COME FOLLOW ME: AND I WILL GIVE YOU REST

YOU SHALL CROSS THE BARREN DESERT

BUT YOU SHALL NOT DIE OF THIRST,

YOU SHALL WONDER FAR IN SAFETY

THOUGH YOU DO NOT KNOW THE WAY.

YOU SHALL SPEAK YOUR WORDS TO FOREIGN

MEN AND THEY WILL UNDERSTAND.

YOU SHALL SEE THE FACE OF GOD AND LIVE.

IF YOU PASS THROUGH RAGING WATERS IN

THE SEA, YOU SHALL NOT DROWN.

IF YOU WALK AMID THE BURNING FLAMES,

YOU SHALL NOT BE HARMED.

IF YOU STAND BEFORE THE POWER OF HELL

AND DEATH IS AT YOUR SIDE; KNOW THAT I AM WITH YOU THROUGH IT
ALL.

BLESSED ARE THE POOR, FOR THE

KINGDOM SHALL BE THEIRS.

BLEST ARE YOU THAT WEEP AND MOURN,

FOR ONE DAY YOU SHALL LAUGH. AND IF

WICKED MEN INSULT AND HATE YOU ALL

BECAUSE OF ME, BLESSED, BLESSED ARE YOU.

At the "kiss of peace", a couple of her artist friends came forward and kissed the casket, a gesture which deeply touched all who observed it. The whole service was filled with that mixture of joy and sorrow we were beginning to become accustomed to. I didn't cry on the outside. Strangely, I had a kind of strength that is difficult to explain. But on the inside, the pain was reaching a stage much like numbness. The consolation was that feeling that Ellen was very near as a matter of fact, I felt as if she were witnessing all of this just as we were.

Everyone was invited back to the house and I only know the house was crowded with people. Here in our home, friends took over in the kitchen and put out food for what must have been hundreds of people. "You satisfy my hungry heart, with gifts of finest wheat."

◆   ◆   ◆

The days that followed were somber, as they must be for all who lose a loved one. Each of us was trying to continue our regular life styles, but there was always heaviness. We were fortunate I guess, because we all felt so free to talk about Ellen. We cherished the things she gave to us and we discussed her almost constantly.

Each day the mailman brought more consolations—gifts to the Leukemia Fund—Spiritual Offerings—Precious messages and a few sent pictures of happier times spent with Ellen. All these were very special to us.

◆   ◆   ◆

About three weeks after the funeral Bill was out in the driveway changing the oil in the car. He came running into the house all excited and preceded to tell me what the excitement was about. It seems that as he was working, changing the filter on the car, his thoughts were of Ellen. As he slid from under the car he looked from beneath the raised hood and his eyes fell on the sculpture, which is on our lawn.

He remembered the day she brought the large metal sculpture home on her truck. He thought to himself, *now what is this and where does she think it's going?*

She asked if she could set it on the lawn and he said he guessed it would be all right, but asked, "What is it?"

"If an artist has to abstract their work, it's no longer art. What do you think it is?"

He looked awhile at this fairly large sized metal structure. Part of it stands about six feet in the shape of a large C. In front of the large C are four stilts and on each stilt is a small C shaped piece. Three of the small Cs face away from the large C, while only one, which stands taller than the other three, faces the large C. Bill answered her question.

He thought the large C could be God's love flowing on His people. The small Cs represented the people, but only a small percentage of them were looking back and returning that love.

"Not bad Dad, not bad," was her only reply.

Now here he was a few years later looking at the sculpture with a very different heart.

The message was right there in the sculpture.

"MANY ARE CALLED BUT FEW ARE CHOSEN."

♦   ♦   ♦

There were other things that happened too. Kathy, George and the children came to see us as often as possible. We all seemed to need each other's support and we needed to talk a lot about Ellen. On this particular day Kathy spoke out with great effort.

"I saw Ellie"

Suddenly everyone was silent and staring at her as she sat uncomfortably. Then she repeated, "I saw Ellie—twice." We all know her not to be one with a big imagination so we waited for the explanation.

She was working around her house, she didn't think she was even thinking of Ellie, when she looked across her living room and saw her standing there. She was wearing jeans, a T-shirt and her hair was long again. She smiled a little and said to Kathy, "Tell mom and dad that everything is alright" and as Kathy stared, Ellen disappeared. Kathy did not feel frightened, just kind of dazed. As she thought about it over and over again she decided she must have imagined the whole episode and decided to say nothing to anyone.

Five or six days after this incident, the exact same thing happened again. This time Kathy felt she must relate the message. She did not know the words Rod had spoken to us in the hospital corridor right after Ellen had died.

"If only she could come back just once and tell us everything's alright."

◆   ◆   ◆

About a week later I picked Grampa up for Mass on a Sunday morning and as usual I asked how he was doing. His answer surprised me as he usually says he's just fine. Instead he said something about guessing he was all right after what happened last night. He refused to tell me what it was that happened, but he did appear to be somewhat shaken up. After Mass we went back to our house as we always did on Sundays. When Bill came home a couple of hours later, I told him of my conversation with his father and suggested he try to find out what upset him. As the day went on Grampa did confide in Bill and later Bill told me.

Grampa was kneeling and praying by his bed. He was praying for Elley when he looked up and saw her face. It was so clear to him that he reached out to touch her but she said, "Don't touch me Grampa, but tell mom and dad that everything is alright."

Then she disappeared.

Grampa had never in his eighty years had such an experience and it did shake him up. It was then that Bill told him of Kathy's experience. He did not know about it before that time.

I thought long and hard about these things. I wondered about the wall or veil that separates us. I knew that night after night I would get out of bed and sit in the living room that contained so many memories of her and secretly wish she would appear to me. It never happened. Now somehow I know, without a doubt that she got her message to us in whatever way she could. I knew that I must wait until I join her before I would ever see her again. I would not go looking for her anymore.

◆   ◆   ◆

Ellen's birthday and Mother's day were practically always celebrated together. They always fell within a few days. In our house it was Mother's day and Ellen's birthday, Father's day and Kathy's birthday. Of course this year the day meant a heavier than usual heart, but one thing pleased me very much. It was the Mother's day card I received from Dennis. Dennis is not generally one to get over emotional, so that gave it even greater meaning. It simply said "Happy Mother's Day" on the outside and when opened, it said, "you're the best." The meaningful part was the poetry he wrote in it, taken from Shakespeare.

> Heaven and yourself
> Had part of this fair maid,
> Now Heaven hath all,
> And all the better it is for the maid.
> Your part in her you could not keep from death,
> But Heaven keeps his part in Eternal Life.

I also have the good fortune to have a Mother's day card that Ellen had made for me the previous year. I'm not one who keeps all the cards, but the special ones I do keep and thank God, this simple little card I felt is very special. In it she wrote:

Dear Mom:

I guess this is the time of year to think about just how lucky or blessed to have you as a mother. I am ever grateful for your love and guidance in this confusing world. Thank you forever, Elley

And this is my Mother's day card from her forever.

All these things bring comfort to the grieving heart, but the mourning and weeping must take its course and we who are left behind, hopefully will be a little more purified because of it.

◆   ◆   ◆

A whole year later I received a phone call from a teacher from Ellen's high school. She had just found out about Ellen's death and was devastated to hear of it. She was trying to get in touch with the first officer's of an organization called SHIP—Students Helping Individual People. Ellen was their first president.

I remembered how it all got started. In the summer after Ellen's junior year in high school, she said to me that she'd like to do some volunteer work with the retarded. I was delighted, so we called the Fernald School for the retarded in Waltham. She could give one day a week, but since she would need a ride and did not yet have her license, I also volunteered a day. We went together and she was assigned to work in the Green Blind Unit with the children. The woman in charge of volunteers asked what I would like to do? I said since I was there basically to be Ellen's transportation, it really didn't matter. She said there was an area where they did need help but no one wanted it because it wasn't working directly with the patients. I said that was all right with me, I'd do it, what was it? In their store area they needed help separating and sorting clothing. So there I was, once a week, surrounded by donated clothes. I had to look up to heaven and say, 0 Lord, I just know my purgatory is going to be folding a huge mountain of clothes. With nine people in the house it seemed washing, sorting folding, ironing was endless. I really began to hate clothes. But it was worth it to see one of the children exercise what we tried to teach them, to give of themselves.

One morning as we drove into the Fernold grounds, we spotted one of the teachers from the high school. She was walking with one of the blind children. We stopped the car and in unison, said to each other, "What are you doing here?"

Obviously she was also donating time and said how nice it would be if more of the high school students did this type of thing. Ellen responded with, "If you want any help getting something started, I'll be a senior class officer next year and I'll be glad to help".

That was the beginning. Miss Smith told me that night on the phone how ten years earlier; Ellen had gone to the school committee and requested funds for a bus to bring students once a week to the Fernald School. The request was granted and the funds re-instated every year since.

The tenth anniversary of this organization was a living tribute to Ellen and the good she left behind.

These are some of the memories I want to hold on to as I continue my journey in this valley of tears. I pray that each time I descend from the mountains and enter the valleys I will remember to reach out and grasp that hand of the Lord's that is always extended to me.

> "Teach me 0 Lord, the secrets of my heart.
> Cast out all fear and fill it with love.
> That on the special day when the veil is lifted,
> I will stand before my love,
> Having "laughed all of my laughter,
> And cried all my tears."

SUMMER ON CAPE COD

PROLOGUE

Your pain is the breaking of the shell that encloses your under-standing
Even as the stone of the fruit must break,
That it's heart may stand in the sun, so must you know pain.—
Pain is the bitter potion by which the physician within you heals your sick self.
Therefore trust the physician, and drink His remedy in silence and tranquility."

Kahlil Gibran/The Prophet

This is the story of six months in a woman's life. I am that woman. In order to better understand the story, the reader needs to understand where I am coming from. I was one of the many children who grew up during the great depression. I came from a loving family. As a child, I never realized how tight money was. Being the youngest of four girls, I wore just about all "hand me downs." My mother had a talent for tell-ing me how beautiful the material was and how lucky I was for getting a sweater from my cousin etc. I believed every word my parents told me and wore my things with pride. I was made to feel pretty and tal-ented. Whether I was, or not, it gave me a sense of confidence that I wanted to pass on to my own children when the time came. I hope I did. Both my husband and I went to parochial school and were trained by the sisters to love God, our religion, and country.

We met in high school. I was 15 and Bill, was 17. World War 2 was going on and all eligible males were taken into the service as soon as they reached 18. Bill was gone for two years. Thank God the war ended while he was in the army, thus allowing the young men to come home. I was in college while he was gone. We wrote to each other all the time. Two years after he came home we married and in the next sixteen years we produced seven children, 4 boys and 3 girls. Money continued to be tight, but I was used to that. Using my mother's formula, the children did not feel deprived. Nor were they deprived. Their father worked two jobs for fourteen years, in order to give all of us a better life. He would leave the house at six in the morning and not return until eleven at night. Weekends were spent doing things with the family. All the children had chores.

Compatible with their age, from emptying the wastebasket to mowing the lawn. One thing they grew up knowing was that they were to go to college after they finished high school. That meant keeping good grades in school. As for the cost, we would cross that bridge as we came to it, managing as we had always done.

As in all large families, we had difficult and sorrowful times as well as joyous times. In the difficult times, such as the death of our second daughter at age 25, after she had just received her Masters Degree in Fine Arts. Leukemia stole her from us. This heartbreak that never ends, was borne only by our strong faith.

Family was the most important mission in our lives. While Bill earned the money for their wants and needs, I did most of the training in the home. We were firm believers in the father being the head and mother being the heart of the family.

Most of the time I enjoyed my children. As the children grew, I worked teaching in the local school system, it afforded me the opportunity of knowing the boys and girls they spent their time with. Their friends were in and out of our house all the time. The children were taught to be frugal and to know that whatever goals they sought, they had our support. Bill kept a firm hand on any "fly by night ideas" any of them might get, and there were some.

We laughed, we argued, we played, and we were a family who knew each other pretty well. When this story opens, the six living children are grown and settled in their life's work. I hope you will enjoy getting to know all of us as you read this story.

"You have a tumor on your brain."

These words are some of the most frightening and startling words one can hear from their doctor. These are the words I heard in the summer of 96. I thought a death sentence had been pronounced, no matter how much the doctor tried to convince me that it was not so.

The National Institute of Health statistics says that new brain tumors arise in more than 40,000 Americans each year. They are most common in middle aged and older adults, with the highest risk being people in their 60s. No one knows the cause of brain tumors. Some things being studied are environments; certain industries such as oil refining, rubber manufacturing and drug manufacturing. Chemists and embalmers seem to have higher incidences of brain tumors.

I tell my story to give hope to people who may have to hear those dreadful words. Truly, some tumors are more dangerous than others, but when I found out I had one, "I had known only two other people who had brain tumors and they were both dead."

It's time spread the word that many survive brain tumor surgery. With medicine, and proper therapy they go on with their lives and count their blessings.

1

SUMMER BEGINS

I sit in the shadow of a pine grove on a knoll over looking Seymour
Lake. It is quiet as a painting with only a breeze rippling the surface
of the water. To my right the old man cups his hands around a match
as he struggles to ignite the barbecue. He wears sandals, shorts and hat
and I think to myself that he still has great legs. Sounds like a funny
thought but I remember fighting the flab on my thighs and jealously
wondering why he had such great legs. Now the jealousy is gone and I
enjoy looking at him and thinking he still looks pretty good for his age.
We have history. Over fifty years of it. More than half a century is a
long time. In my reveries I think of the many years. If I were to write
down all of the interesting things over those years, it would take vol-
umes. It would cover joyful events, sad times when love abounded and
times when it seemed we should end it all. We couldn't even seem to
have a compatible thought. We laughed, we cried, we argued, we made
up. After it all, here we are still together and after seven children, here
we are alone, all by ourselves, having our private little picnic.

It's September and summer is just about over. We're taking advantage of every good day we get before old man winter really sets in to
stay.

Last year we bought a second hand Old Town canoe, a little electric
motor, life jackets and all the gear to get out on those lakes and snag
some really nice trout. We also bought a couple of bikes. Not the fancy
racing type but the kind we rode as kids. Balloon tires, single speed.
We had wonderful times on them. First riding around a park and cemetery near home to see if we remembered how to ride. Eventually we

49

were brave enough to venture on some back streets down near the beach. Finally we bought a bike rack and we'd pack a small lunch and head for the trails here on Cape Cod. One day we must have traveled twenty miles. We were getting pretty agile hopping on and off those bikes with ease. By the end of the summer we were considering turning the bikes in for ones with speeds, but then decided to put the decision off until this year.

This year turned out to be a little different. We arrived anxiously on the Cape in late May. The weather hadn't warmed up enough to swim in the lakes and the ocean was still icy as winter snow. We were not about to risk going in. We spent time visiting with our children, eating too much and getting fatter, making annual doctor appointments and other mundane things.

On May 31st we went to Hyannis, about a fifteen-minute ride from home. There is a beauty school there and I needed a haircut. My hair has a natural curl and if I get a good cut it requires practically no care. A young girl started cutting my hair and as soon as she began I knew I had a real novice. What can I expect at a beauty school? The instructors watch them so carefully that there is usually no problem. When they start separating your hair into small compartments you know you have a real beginner. "oh gee," I thought, "This will take forever." No sooner had the thought crossed my mind than I began getting strange feelings coming up in my body. Then I began to sweat and feel weak. How I wanted to lie down. I said to the girl, "I feel weak so she had better stop cutting for awhile."

The poor girl got more nervous than I was and asked, "Could I get you a glass of water?"

I shook my head "yes."

Seeing me visibly sweating she suggested we move to the back room where it was cooler. I agreed and pulled myself together enough to follow her. I sat and drank my water. The slight breeze coming in the back door made me feel a little better so I said to her, "Go ahead and finish the haircut."

She started to continue her job and the next thing I remembered was opening my eyes and seeing the instructor, three more workers and Bill staring at me. I knew I must have passed out but I didn't feel weak or miserable any more, I just felt like a fool for causing such a commotion.

"Are you all right?" Each one in turn asked.

"I'm fine now."

I heard the instructor whisper to my husband, "911?"

I was so grateful when I heard him say, "No, I'll wait and see how she feels in awhile."

The instructor came over and finished the haircut in about two minutes flat. It turned out to be one of the best haircuts I had in a long time. I'm sure she couldn't wait to get me out of the place. I really did feel fine. I was able to get up and tip my young girl and go to the desk and pay my bill.

Bill and I went out to the car and before I had a chance to thank him for not letting her call 911, he announced to me that he was taking me to the emergency room at the Cape Cod Hospital. I vehemently protested, but he wouldn't answer me and kept driving to the hospital that was only about five minutes away. I was furious, claiming I wouldn't go in, there was nothing wrong with me, etc. etc.

I tried to make light of the matter in front of the doctor but Bill was right there saying he saw me "out cold" in the chair at the beauty parlor. I had blood tests, X-rays, cardiogram and a heart monitor attached to me. I had to lie for several hours having a nurse come to check the monitor periodically. I was not happy. Finally I was given permission to leave providing I wore a 24 hour heart monitor and would see my doctor at MGH (man's greatest hospital} in Boston within two days. At that point I would have consented to anything to get out of there. To make matters worse, the E.R. doctor was very concerned about the chest X-ray. One part of it looked shaded and I was to bring it with me to Mass General. His concern began to worry me just a little and all the way home I had to listen to, "Aren't you glad I made you see a doctor?"

My evening was ruined. I was wrong about not wanting to get checked for my tiny fainting spell and now I had to worry that something might really be wrong with me. That very day I called to make an appointment in Boston. I got one for two days later. The next day Bill returned the 24-hour monitor to the hospital. When I heard nothing about it I assumed all was well in that area.

My doctor at MGH gave me another thorough going over, emphasizing my heart and having me repeat the X-ray while comparing the new X-ray with older ones. She has been my doctor for nearly a decade so she knows me pretty well. She went to medical school and did her residency with one of our sons so I always feel kind of special. Sometimes I feel too special, in that any complaints I've had in the past resulted in in-depth examining and testing. The tests always turned out negative. In other words, I'm a pretty healthy old gal. Now I feel like I must sound like a hypochondriac when I make little complaints. That little bout of passing out in the beauty parlor was so brief and I've felt so perfect since, I really hoped she would say, "We'll forget it for now and watch to see if it happens again." But lo—she didn't. Since the new X-ray looked fine, she explained, "Sometimes Helen, when a portable machine is used (as it was in the E.R.) The sitting position often could cause the blood vessels to kind of bunch up and they look like a mass in the picture."

The lungs being cleared, she then concentrated on the heart. She knew from my medical history that my father had died of a heart attack at 62 and most of his family died of heart problems. I had already beaten that age and was still going strong.

"You know 24 hours of heart monitoring is insufficient in your case so I want you to wear a monitor day and night for at least 30 days."

"What! I don't like this at all."

We had our little polite argument, me claiming that I felt fine and didn't want my summer ruined.

"You can take it off to go for a swim as long as you wear it all the rest of the time. It's really very simple. If you have a weak spell or any unusual feelings you simply dial a phone number and lay the monitor on the phone and the results will be sent to me."

Modern technology! It was going to drive me nuts. Almost prophetic thoughts, but I didn't know it at the time. As usual she won the argument and I consented to wear the monitor.

"I'll order it today day but it might be a couple of weeks before you receive it, so call me if you have any spells."

I didn't express my thought to her but they were clearly that I must take advantage of my two weeks freedom.

I left the office pleasant and smiling and greeted my waiting husband growling and complaining. Of course he took the doctor's side.

"Look how lucky you are. She didn't just brush you off but insisted on finding your problem."

We bantered back and forth me saying I didn't have a problem and him saying I did and the doctor is right to try to find it.

That night, "my son the doctor" called to see how I made out. The expression, "my son the doctor" has become a joke in our house ever since he graduated from medical school some 10 years before. Tuft's University had a general graduation with speeches and all the formalities shared by all the different graduating schools. After that part, all graduate schools were separated to different areas of the campus where they would hear a speaker directed to their field of study and receive their diplomas. The Medical School had the honor of being in front of the president's house. Our family was seated about three-quarters of the way back in the group of all parents and friends of the new doctors. After the speech it was time for the diplomas, the moment these young people had looked forward to for four long years. As names were called one by one they went up to the podium, received their diploma, then filed down the center isle passing friends and families. Everyone was very proud. Bill leaned over to me and whispered, "Here comes your son the doctor." Bursting with pride myself, I laughed and said out loud, "Here's my son the doctor."

Everyone in our area heard me and they laughed and clapped. After all I was simply expressing the thoughts of just about everyone there. I have a picture I hold very dear in memory of that special day. It's of three of our sons, with Rod in the middle in his graduation gown with the green trim signifying Medical School, Donald the youngest on one side and Scott seven years younger than Rod on the other. Scott said as the picture was being taken, "That'll be me in seven years."

No one even suspected Scott was thinking of Medical School at that time, but sure enough seven years later we repeated that prideful moment.

Well anyway, "my son the doctor" called to hear how I made out at my doctor's appointment. I told him and complained about having to wear the heart monitor for a month. He patiently explained that there are certain types of heart problems that do not show up in a regular check up or even on an E.K.G. I didn't say it to him, but we've all heard of the person who got a complete bill of health one day from their doctor and the next day had a heart attack. Rod went on to say that since there are so many heart problems on his Grampa's side of the family it made sense to order long term monitoring for me. I had to promise him that I would be sure to call in any dizzy or weak spells I might get. I felt a little "ganged up" on, but Rod always had a way with me that I couldn't say no to him.

Weather wise this was not the greatest summer on Cape Cod. It's been cooler with more rain than usual. When we did have good hot summer days we would go to Scargo Lake. It's a very beautiful place. The blue lake surrounded by pine trees is as something in a storybook. It's only a mile from our home but in the opposite direction from the ocean. We would swim all over the lake with no fear of being hit by a boat as only small boats and canoes are allowed on the lake. Last year with much coaxing from Bill, I swam all the way across the lake with him. The spring fed water makes your skin feel silky smooth as if covered with moisturizing lotion. I would float and look at the clouds form all kinds of interesting figures as the sea gulls swooped across them. After spending an afternoon like that I'd be more relaxed than if I had a double martini before dinner. I looked forward to doing much more of the same thing this year, but so far the weather was against us. On cloudy or rainy days we would shop or visit friends or do some work in the house. We only got to the lake about twice in the next two weeks and only for a short time.

One of the days when it was sunny but cool, around the second week of June, I wanted to get the old bikes out and ride down to the ocean. Bill didn't feel like going bike riding but I nagged and finally said, "Well I'm going anyway."

He finally consented. He got the bikes out of the shed and I attached my bike bag to the handlebars and put a couple of cans of tonic in it. I put my funny Klaxon horn near the handle to send signals to my bike mate. We geared up with our helmets and were on our way. I thought how lucky we were to be in the middle of the beach and the lake. It felt great to pedal down the narrow, winding road. With the breeze blowing against my face, I felt like the luckiest person in the world. I felt young again. At the end of the almost empty parking lot there is an incline covered with gravel leading up to a grassy area behind the sand dunes. There are benches and picnic tables where we sat after parking our bikes. This area overlooked the ocean and I felt like I was in a south sea island brochure. We sat drinking our cans of tonic and absorbing the scenery. Lifeguards were further behind us getting their instructions in preparation for the official opening of the beach with its onslaught of summer visitors. Everything seemed beautiful. Bill even said, "You know this was a good idea to bike down here."

I just gave him a victorious look. We spent about two hours enjoying the crisp, cool afternoon. It was close to 5 P.M. when I said, "You know we better head back home."

He agreed. We walked back to where we parked our bikes and put our helmets back on. Bill said, "Watch out at the bottom of the decline because I think they put a chain across it around 4 o'clock."

I started down before him and it was wide open. I turned my head to holler back that there was no chain up, when my bike skid on the gravel and I went flying off into the stony ground. I knew immediately that my right ankle or leg was hurt. My arms and face were scraped from the gravel. Bill jammed on his brakes and hopped off his bike to come over to me as I was getting myself up.

"Are you all right?"

"Yes, I think so, but my right ankle might be sprained. I'm going to get it into the cold ocean water."

I took off my shoes and began to hobble down through the sand into the water.

"Are you able to walk on it?"

I felt like a little kid for falling off a bike. I tried to make light of it.

"Oh yes, I think it's just a slight sprain. The cold water will keep it from swelling too much."

The cold ocean waters immediately felt good on my leg and I just walked in it for about ten minutes. A little boy catching tiny crabs came up to me and asked if I'd hold his pail while he searched by the rocks. As I held the pail, he hurried back and forth adding more crabs to his collection. By the time he took his pail back I decided I was probably able to walk on the leg. I headed towards the shore and up through the sand but with each step I had to favor the leg a little more. Bill, seeing the situation came towards me to help.

"You're not going to be able to ride that bike up the hill," I had to agree.

"I'll go home and get the car, you wait right here near your bike. It won't take me very long."

He got on his bike and started the uphill ride. Fifteen or twenty minutes later he arrived back in the car. He didn't take time to put the bike rack on thinking he could put my bike in the trunk or back seat, but no matter how he manipulated, it just didn't fit in. Then he went looking for a tool to remove one wheel, but wouldn't you know, there was none. Finally he looked at me and said, "Is your foot good enough to drive the car?"

"Oh sure, I can drive."

"Good, then you drive the car home and I'll ride your bike." "O.K. I'll see you at home."

He started up the hill before me but I soon passed him struggling away on a seat much too low and handlebars too near his knees. He arrived exhausted about ten minutes after me and immediately started the old, "I'll take you to the emergency room."

I couldn't help but think *here we go again.* I also thought of having been there two weeks earlier, getting all kinds of heart checks and being sent home with a monitor. My thoughts were that the doctor would think, "This woman is crazy. Now she's out bike riding and falls off." There was no way I was going back to that emergency room. The argument began again. I insisted that it's just a sprain and I'll be fine in a day or two. Bill was too tired to fight with me.

"O.K. You tell ME when you're ready to go."

I put ice on the leg and hopped for the rest of the evening, taking aspirin for pain.

The first thing I heard the next morning was, "Well are you ready to go to the emergency room yet?"

I hated to give in and so I remained stubborn.

I could still hobble around and spend the day catering to my leg. I could sit and keep it elevated and iced and be waited on a little. By evening Bill was totally disgusted with me. I knew that when he said, "O.K., I'm not going to say another word but you'll regret not taking care of it."

I just pooh, poohed him and claimed it was already getting better.

The next day was Sunday, Father's Day. The phone rang early and it was Kathy, our oldest daughter, and saying that she and her husband would be down to take us to dinner for Father's Day. I didn't mention my fall and said we'd be looking for them. Bill said, "How are you going out to a restaurant?"

"I can walk, I'll just lean on you a little."

They arrived around noontime. Kathy stood tall and slender in the doorway, her long brown hair surrounding eyes and mouth expressing shock in seeing my condition. Then came the obvious question, "What happened to you?"

Before I could get a word in edgewise, Bill said, "Your mother fell off her bike and won't let me take her to the emergency room."

"It's just a sprain," I chimed in.

My daughter who is a nurse (I don't know where we got this medical family! Whenever I call one of them with a complaint they always seem to ask if I saw my doctor?) Said, "Let me take a look at it mom."

She came over to me at the far end of the living room, sat beside me, and started looking and gently touching the leg. She whispered to me, "You really should get this X-rayed."

"shh don't let your father hear you."

She gave me a little perturbed look and said out laud, "Can you put any weight on it?"

"Oh sure, I can walk, where do you want to go for dinner."

We went off to a local restaurant. My walking was being done with Bill on one side and George, a giant of a man, on the other. It was a great way to celebrate Father's Day, but by the time we got back to the house and I got into my lounge chair and was able to elevate my leg, Kathy came over and sat close to me. In a low voice she said, "Promise me Mom that you'll see about that tomorrow. You know at your age you could get blood clots."

My leg was hurting enough at that point that I agreed that I would.

The next morning we were off to the E.R. and lucky me got Dr. Jefferson again. He took one look and ordered an X-ray. If he recognized me he was kind enough not to mention it for which I was very grateful. I waited on a gurney for the results, still convinced that it would be just a sprain. A short time later the doctor came back, X-ray in hand and said to the nurse something about putting an elastic stocking on me and an air cast and having me get an appointment with a doctor Coin in two weeks. Turning to me he said, "You have a break in your leg."

Before he could finish what he was saying I butt in with, "It can't be broken, I don't believe it!"

Without a word he went for the X-ray and brought it to me.

"See that bone, that's the fibula, see that line across it?" I sheepishly said, "yes."

"Well that's where the break is. Make an appointment with Dr. Coin in two weeks, he's an orthopedic doctor, meantime keep the cast on and we'll give you a prescription for pain and a cane to help keep the weight off of it."

He said it all so authoritatively that I was as a child taking instructions from daddy. It had been at least thirty years since I broke two-foot bones while skiing. I thought I was invulnerable to that stuff by now. But no! Reality was beginning to dawn as I got all braced up to leave there with Bill on one side and a cane on the other listening to, "Didn't I tell you?"

Heaven help me. It was the beginning of my summer vacation.

2

ANOTHER SETBACK

We filled our bellies with steak, beans and salad, all prepared by my lover of 48 years. When all the clearing up was done, he retired to the hammock and I to my favorite spot where I amused myself watching the birds. Chickadees, finch, gulls swooping over the lake like angels in a fairy tale. On the ground I watched squirrels, both gray and red, small chip monks who almost ran over my feet. How wonderful to sit in total silence. The creatures of nature don't even realize I'm here as they go about their daily routine and I get to watch at close range. Look at that squirrel! He spotted me and ran behind a tree. Now! Only minutes later, as a child plays peek-a-boo, I see his little face peeking around the tree to see if I'm still here. I've disturbed his normal stomping grounds so he decides to leave me far behind by ascending the tree. Nature is entertaining me and I think to myself that it would never be like this if it were my normal summer. I'd be off on the bike trails or walking the beach on such a beautiful fall day.

A broken leg was going to mess up six weeks of my summer I learned, as I obediently made and kept the appointment with Doctor Coin. He stood about 5 foot nine. His face was round and he wore horn-rimmed glasses giving him a look of serene seriousness. He smiled and explained what would take place. Again my leg was X-rayed. He showed me how the bone was already beginning to heal and calcium was building over the injured area. I suppose I was encouraged but still I knew half the summer would be over before I could be really active. I wanted to bring grand children to the beach and have fun as a child myself. Instead I sat around the house perhaps getting out to lunch or an early bird special with Bill, who tried to think up places to take me in the car to occupy our days. All the while I'm aware that the darn monitor would be arriving any day and it would have to be added to my cast and cane. Talk about feeling old. I kept bemoaning the fact that I probably wouldn't be able to ride my bike until fall. Bill's answer irritated me. He always came back with that sing song, "to the dump, to the dump, to the dump, dump, dump."

There was one thing we did that I enjoyed. We lived very close to the oldest playhouse in the country, Cape Cod Playhouse. Every year we buy season tickets. I have a friend from childhood her name is Mae. She lives on the Cape too but on the other side, in Falmouth. A few years ago we both decided to get tickets to the playhouse. That would be our way of making sure we got together at least 6 or 7 times over the course of the summer. I had to chuckle to myself as I thought of the events that were brought about a year ago as a result of our friendship.

Mae, a thin, wiry woman with a constant smile, has a brother named Ben, who was a friend of Bill's even before Mae and I met. As a matter of fact, Bill and I met in their house back when we were in high school. After the death of Ben's wife, several years ago, he became somewhat of a recluse. Mae worries about him and keeps checking on him making sure he takes his medications, eats properly, etc. While their continuing saga was going on we were spending our winters in Florida, so I would only catch up with our old friends through a few phone calls during the winter. Well, one fine day two winters ago, my phone rang. The person on the other end said, "Ellie, this is Bea, Pam gave me your phone number. Do you remember me from college?"

I was so taken back that I lied and said, "of course I do." "Well I'm renting a condo for three months down here in Florida so Pam said I should call you and maybe we could get together." "That would be great," I continued my usual polite conversation. "Maybe you could make it over here for lunch some day?"

"That would be fine," she replied, "I don't know anyone down here."

Our conversation went on and we set a lunch date for the following week and I gave her detailed directions to our condo. I hung up the phone and said to my husband, "I just invited an old college friend to lunch next week, I haven't seen her in over 40 years and I can't even remember what she looked like."

"How'd you get yourself into that he retorted?"

"Pam gave her our number. She's vacationing in Melbourne."

We both knew Pam since high school but I've seen little of her in recent years. I must remember to thank her, I thought sarcastically.

The day arrived and I watched for her Buick station wagon. She had told me I'd recognize it because there'd be a big dog in the back. Here's my out, I thought to myself. "Oh good heavens," I said, "no animals are allowed in our building." And that was the truth. "Oh don't worry," was her reply, "he's old and just eats and sleeps. He'll just lie in the back of the car while we visit. I always bring his water bowl and just leave the windows open." So there I was looking from the balcony for a blue Buick station wagon with a big dog inside. When I saw the car pull into our driveway I asked Bill to go down to open the door and introduce himself, direct her to a shady place to park, for the poor dogs sake and usher her up to our apartment.

We greeted each other with hugs and smiles like old buddies. I still couldn't really remember her. Only her name seemed familiar. The three of us spent the first hour having drinks and appetizers and reminiscing about other old friends we had in common. We all came from the same area of Cambridge, Massachusetts. We were really having fun as both Bill and I had memories of just about all the people she talked about. Bea is a vivacious person who keeps in touch with just about everyone. She brought us up to date on who had died and what was going on with others that were still kicking around like ourselves. Like a hooked fish thrown back in the water, I was feeling real comfortable with Bea. We sat down to lunch and there wasn't one lull in the conversation. She helped clear the dishes. We helped walk the dog. Back inside the talk continued like pages of family photo albums being turned, our minds reviewed the years. Suppertime came and we ate again. The dog got fed and walked again. Oh, if only kids were so easy to care for. She left at 10:30 that night. A ten-hour visit was more fun than a day at Disney. You might say that that's how Bea and I met, because I hardly remember the meeting some 40 something years ago. We got together a few more times during her three-month stay and by the time she left the area, I knew her quite well.

The following summer when we got to Cape Cod and were able to spend some time with our friends Mae and Ben, we really thought Ben had failed. Talking to Mae about him we realized Mae was very upset. She couldn't get him to go anywhere or participate in life. She was really afraid she'd go into his house and find him dead on the floor one of these days. When the four of us were together, we asked him if he would like to meet a friend who is widowed. She remembered him from our younger days. He shook his head, no, but by the time we got home there was a call from Mae who said her brother surprised her by saying that maybe he would like to meet this lady. Now the fun really began. I called Bea to ask if she'd like to renew old acquaintance with Ben. She asked me a barrage of questions about him.

"He was real good looking when he was young, how does he look now?"

"Old like the rest of us," I answered.

"You know what I mean. Bill aged nicely, does he look as good as Bill?"

"They could be brothers," I said sarcastically. On and on it went, but we finally set a date that the four of us would go out to lunch. Then the phone started ringing on the other end. It was my friend Mae filling me in on all Ben's questions. As the time for the date drew near, Bill and I were getting really nervous. Bill started saying that fixing people up was not a great idea. Especially when those people are pushing 70. I felt that we were all acting like we were 16 again, fixing up a blind date.

He arrived three quarters of an hour early, dressed in tan pants and polo shirt, not exactly dressed to the nines, but then he never was one for clothes. She arrived one half hour late, looking just perfect in a nice pantsuit, jewelry, and proper make up, the works. "They're too different for this to work," we were both thinking. So there we were trying to act like everything was normal and we were about as nervous as the two of them were. We really don't change no matter how old we get. Here we were mature people acting like teenagers.

We had a great lunch and everyone calmed down and seemed to enjoy each other's company. They came back to our house and stayed for several hours just gabbing. I was thinking, why doesn't he ask for her phone number? About 6:30 Bea said she had a long drive and should be leaving. Here was his chance to ask for her number, but he never took it. He left about a half-hour after Bea saying what a great day he had. The phone rang two minutes later and it was Mae of course. Anxious to hear all the details, I told her that they both seemed to be enjoying each other but he never did ask for her phone number.

"What is wrong with that stupid brother of mine, give me her number."

So I gave it to her. The follow up became phone calls between the two of them, dates, shopping and whatever. They had a great time for the rest of the summer. I came in one day to get the following message on my machine. "This is the daily update from Falmouth. He's definitely going to dinner with you at Pam and Joe's house. He's going to buy new shoes. He's going to Florida with her. Stay tuned for the latest bulletin. You'll be informed. Talk to you later". I laughed out loud. We were back in high school again.

◆　　　◆　　　◆

I had been wrapped in a cast for over two weeks when the monitor arrived. It was a confusing mess to figure out. I had to dial a certain number on the phone to get it started, registered or whatever they called it. It had to be wired to me in four places. I couldn't do it by myself so Bill had to wire me up. I looked like I was carrying around a six-shooter. I was a cross between being ready to cry and just plain hitting something or someone. I was a very unhappy camper, as the saying goes.

One week later our youngest son and his bride of less than a year came from New York to visit his poor invalid mother. This lifted my spirits somewhat because he was always so busy he seldom had time for visits and I was anxious to spend some time with my new daughter in law. I very much wanted to get to know her as I did my other in-law children. We had a nice weekend with them that passed all too quickly. They presented me with a nice big box of Godiva chocolates. (He knows I'm a chocoholic.) The box was wrapped in a pretty blue ribbon and a sprig of colorful flowers. It was almost too pretty to open, but I managed to get by that obstacle. Fortunately I saved the trimmings knowing they'd come in handy for something, but never dreaming I'd use them for the purpose they came to serve.

The following week I had another appointment with my doctor. She was like a detective still working on the mystery of my dizzy spells. Of course since I'd been wearing my six-shooter I didn't even feel a little bit weak. On Tuesday, July 2nd I kept my appointment. She checked me out and asked me a million questions.

"Think back, did you have any type of weak feelings when you were in Florida?"

I did remember a few incidents that I didn't consider important, but she wanted all the details.

"Well, sometimes when I'd be making breakfast I'd get feelings that would make me think that if I didn't lay down I'd fall down, so I'd just go in the bedroom and lay on the bed. The feeling would pass in less than five minutes and I felt perfect again. Sometimes I would wonder what I had eaten or drank the night before that might have caused it. Once I felt perfect again I just forgot about it. Bill never even knew I had left the room. As a matter of fact once I told him I could drop dead on the floor and he wouldn't even notice. I don't think he knew what I was talking about. I told you that if I could have laid down in the beauty parlor I would have been fine."

Then she hit me with a beauty of a statement.

"There's just one more thing that I want you to do, and that's to see a neurologist."

"Oh no, not another doctor."

"This is different, this doctor specializes in dizziness, and we call him the dizzy doctor."

I had to laugh but I still didn't want to see him.

"I don't want to make another trip from the cape, besides, I feel like a hypochondriac, seeing all these doctors, wearing this monitor and everything else, and I always check out just fine."

"Just one visit is all I'll ask you to make. In that way we've at least made a contact with him in case we need him in the future."

I reluctantly gave in. She always seemed to win.

The next week I had to go to see Dr. Coin again about my leg. Again he X-rayed it and found it continuing to heal. He said I didn't have to use the cane unless I felt I needed it. I didn't tell him that I hardly ever used it in the past week or so but I felt I had to make it look like I was obeying all his orders going to his office. I asked when I would get rid of the cast, and he said it would be a minimum of six weeks. I was to see him in another month. As soon as we arrived back home I headed for the calendar hanging in the kitchen and marked six weeks from the time the cast went on. I could feel Bill's eyes giving me that disgusted look he's so good at, but neither of us said a word.

The one good thing we did that week was to go to the Playhouse. My friend from Falmouth came over and up-dated us on the romance. It was still going strong and her brother had again entered the world of the living. Why they even went dancing! They were having a lot better summer than we were.

The dizzy doctor visit came two days later. That was an experience. After I answered the same questions everyone else had asked even though he had those answers in a folder right in front of him, he still had to hear all the answers for himself. Then he took me to his examining room where I went through the craziest testing I had ever had. He put me through all kinds of gyrations to make me feel dizzy, checking my eyes through some kind of machine in both light and dark. The dark was made possible by placing some kind of cloth over my head that was real light proof, but because of the electrical hook ups; he could see my eye reactions on a machine. It's difficult to describe. After about an hour of all this stuff, I still felt fine. Just as I expected. He sent for Bill to come into the office and explained to both of us that he basically found nothing to cause these spells I got. He did however want me to get an MRI. All I could think of was that they always seem to want one more thing. Again I complained about the trip to Boston and any other excuse I could think of. He claimed he just wanted the blood vessels going into my brain checked and he could send me to a place that would cut the trip in half. Of course with Bill there I had no way of getting out of it. The doctor had his secretary make the appointment right then. Lucky for me it wouldn't be for about ten days. Ten days where I only had to put up with a cast and a heart monitor.

3

STARTLING ANNOUNCEMENT

Weather permitting; we went to the lake. I sat on a beach chair while Bill had a nice long swim. I decided it was too much trouble to take off my cast and elastic stocking and all the other gear on me to bother going into the water. Another day we brought friends here, where we are now, for a cook out. This place belongs to our son Rod and his wife Alice. It's their "get away." The attraction for them is the isolation. Rod met Alice when he was in college. He went to Brandies University, which is primarily a Jewish college. I remember Bill saying to me, "Don't be surprised if he brings home a Jewish girl friend." Surprisingly enough, he didn't. He brought home an oriental girl friend. Rod and Alice were married when he was in medical school. They have given us a key to their "hide away" to use anytime we want to. Since we live in a condo, we don't have the advantage of a back yard for things like cookouts. This is much better than just a back yard; here we have a nice lake and all the facilities of a home. During my ten days of semi freedom, we are taking advantage of this lovely place.

I started to chuckle to myself and Bill said, "What are you laughing at?"

"I thought you were asleep. I'm just sitting here reminiscing." Actually I was thinking of a funny incident that happened at our dinner table almost twenty years ago. The two oldest were married, one to a polish girl and the other to a French fellow. Only five of the children were around the table. It must have been some holiday weekend because Rod was in medical school and engaged to Alice and our second daughter was in graduate school and they were both there. While we were eating, our daughter said, "Dad, what would you say if I told you I'm dating a Jewish guy?" Bill put down his silverware, sat bolt upright; his eyes surfed the five offspring before him and said, "What do you kids think I'm running here? The League of Nations!"

Everyone burst out laughing. Even Bill had a smirk on his lips as he picked up his folk to continue eating, looked at his daughter and said in a soft voice, "Just make sure he's a nice guy."

◆　　　◆　　　◆

I seemed to be getting quite a few of those feelings of nausea for no apparent reason, especially in the mornings. I was darn sure I wasn't pregnant, not at my age. Bill suggested I push the button on the monitor when that happened and call the number that records the heart readings. I figured I might as well send something in since Dr. Candie had said to monitor any strange feelings. Anyway I had only about two more weeks and the cast would be off and shortly before that I'd get rid of the monitor. I couldn't wait. I'd be free at last! Free at last!

◆　　　◆　　　◆

On the date I had scheduled the MRI, we headed out in the morning and in only one hour and fifteen minutes we found the place. It was a very modern medical facility. As we stepped inside I recognized that section on the lower level as one that was used for physical therapy. We went up a short staircase to a waiting room that was for people getting MRIs. I checked in, and the receptionist explained that the MRI would take forty-five minutes to an hour. If I wanted the results to go to any doctor besides the one who ordered the test I could fill out a card. I filled out a card for Dr. Candie so she would also have a copy of the results. After a short wait *I* was ushered into one of the more intimidating rooms. A very personable girl explained everything that would take place. She went on to tell me that periodically I would hear banging sounds so not to let it bother me. Let's get it over with, were my thoughts, but I listened politely. Of course I had to explain the cast on my leg and watch the usual laughter when I said

"I fell off my bike."

My head was set in a kind of plastic cage that prevented me from moving it in any direction. By the time she had me set so she could slide the table I lay on into the machine, I was as a person in a straight jacket. I was logically telling myself that it made sense, which I guess it does, but at the same time I hated the feeling of being so restrained. A microphone was somewhere inside playing music to calm me and I could hear the technician's instructions to me. For the first time in my life I discovered that I must be claustrophobic. I didn't dare open my eyes for fear of trying to sit up, escape or just scream. Finally after about twenty minutes I had to tell her of my feelings. She passed in something for me to hold, like a little ball, saying that it sometimes helps people to distract their minds. Shortly after that she slid me forward, or the machine back, I'm not sure which. It felt good to come out of that tunnel. She injected me with something that I assume was to enhance the blood vessels more clearly. She asked if I felt well enough to continue. I said, "Yes." I was extremely anxious to get this behind me. I lay with my eyes closed fiddling with the ball and praying that this would end fast. It eventually did end and I was told what a great job I did, an expression I find annoying because it makes me feel like I'm being treated like a small child. I knew nothing derogatory was intended. The test was over and in five days I could remove the cast. The calendar was marked. Things were looking up.

Two days later, on the 26th of July, I packed up the monitor as the instructions advised and brought it to the post office, never so happy to say good-bye to anything, I shipped it back. Three days later I took the air cast off my leg for good. I still had one more appointment with Dr. Coin and Bill thought I should continue to wear the cast until the doctor gave it the official O.K. But I said, "Six weeks and that's how long I wore it."

Sometimes I don't think Bill thinks I'm too sensible. But then again, sometimes I think he's too sensible. Maybe that's why we're good for each other, each pulling the other back to center.

We were into August now and I tried to forget the whole first part of the summer, get rid of my resentment and start enjoying what was left of it. It was the first time I could get all dressed up to go to the play instead of having to wear some loose top to cover the monitor and a sensible shoe on the foot that was working right and any old thing I could find to fit over the other foot that had the cast on it. I felt great. I had a couple of other fun things to look forward to also. My granddaughter was to be married in the middle of October, so that would keep us here on the Cape at least until then. Of course I had to listen to Bill complain that it would be cold by then and why do people pick cold weather to be married, but I didn't pay any attention to that. I was glad because I love New England in the fall, with the trees all beautiful colors and the air brisk. I always called it football weather. The part of watching our favorite teams play football took the curse off it for Bill and I knew that.

Mae came over the following Wednesday. We both got all dressed up for the play and Bill, Mae and I went out to dinner to a local restaurant near the playhouse. Then we were off to the theater. At intermission our friend Pam came running up to us. She and her husband usually went on a different night but happened to have changed their tickets to Wednesday that particular week. Since we live so near the theater, I invited her and her husband back to our house for cake and coffee after the show.

Back at the house we were all gabbing and catching up on each other's lives, Pam told me she had had a call from the president of our high school graduating class about planning a 50th reunion. She was to have a group at her house the next week and asked if I would come.

"Yes, I'd love to help with the arrangements."

I marked the date on the calendar. We spent the next hour discussing where the years had gone. How could we be out of high school for fifty years? Maybe we were a little prejudiced but we all agreed we seemed too young to be out of high school that long. As they all left I felt like my summer was just beginning. There'd be a shower for my granddaughter coming up, her wedding, and a 50th class reunion. This night turned out to be a real "up" for me.

Each day from that time on we managed to get out of the house and do things we had wanted to do all summer. Why even the weather was cooperating. Bill still wouldn't give in on riding our bikes and thought I was out of my mind for even mentioning it. There still was one appointment to keep with Dr. Coin. I knew it would be the last but Bill kept reminding me of it, especially when I would suggest we go for a little bike ride. When we came in from one of our expeditions the following Friday there was a message on the answering machine from Dr. Candie. She said she'd get back to me later. I don't know why but I didn't give it a second thought. On Saturday when we came into the house there was another message from Dr. Candie. This time she said, "We have to talk about your MRI."

I briefly thought to myself, I hope there's nothing wrong. I didn't tell Bill about the message or about my thoughts and I tried to convince myself that she just wanted me to know all was well. Somehow I managed to forget about the whole thing. On Sunday night we were sitting watching TV when at about 9:50 the phone rang. I remember the time because it was just nearing the end of a show we were enjoying. I said to Bill, "Who the heck is calling at this hour?"

I reluctantly went to the kitchen to answer the phone. It was Dr. Candie calling from Colorado; she had just started her vacation.

"Did you hear from Dr. O'Brien?"

He is the dizzy doctor who ordered the MRI.

"No,"

"Your MRI results arrived in my mail on Friday just before I was leaving for my vacation and I've been trying to reach you ever since."

I could feel my heart beginning to beat a little faster thinking I must have some kind of a blockage in my blood vessels or something. I sat on a stool at the breakfast bar and her next question was

"Are you sitting down?"

Now my body began to feel tense and sweaty.

"Yes."

"Helen, You have a tumor on your brain."

My heart raced and I began to tremble. I could not believe what I was hearing.

"What!" I shrieked.

At that Bill heard me and went running for the extension phone in the bedroom. Then I added, "Dr. Candie, that must be a mistake."

"I'm afraid it's not a mistake."

"Well if it is, I'll never go to another doctor as long as I live."

"I wouldn't blame you," she replied in her calm, peaceful voice. Then she added, "but the good news is that yours is a good kind of tumor. It can be removed and I've already made an appointment for you with a Neuro surgeon at 11 o'clock tomorrow morning. Dr. O'Brien will call you and explain more about it to you. He understands these things much better than I do. I'll be in touch with him as soon as I hang up the phone."

Bill took all the information about the neuro surgeon and as she was telling him that she'd call tomorrow night to find out how we made out, he told her to call our son Rod's house because we'd probably be there. We both hung up the phones and Bill came out to the kitchen. We stared at each other in disbelief. No tears. We were just in some kind of state of numbness, and then he put his arms around me and held me tight. I could feel the strength in those arms. Those same strong arms that consoled me so many times throughout the years. When we were young and in our twenties his arms were put through the test of time.

I was expecting our second child. Our first was born on the exact day that the doctor had named as a due date. Somehow I got the idea that it would be the same for the second. A week before my due date I was awake most of the night with pain. In those days women hated the thought of going to the hospital with what we called "false labor" and being sent home. I was convinced that that was what was happening to me, just false labor. Bill was asleep, but in the wee hours of the morning, he heard me groan. He woke up and one look at me and he knew it was time. "I'll time your pain," trying to be helpful. In the state I was in I found it very irritating to have him checking me with a watch and I started to argue that it would all stop because I wasn't due for another week. He started putting things in a bag to take to the hospital and that made me even angrier, so I said, "I'm not going." Looking back, I can't imagine what was wrong with me. Bill got on the phone to call my mother who was going to mind our other child while I was in the hospital. The plan was that my brother-in-law, who lived with my mother and sister, would bring her to our house. We lived only a short distance away. He would then drive Bill and me to the hospital. Bill was trying to get some clothes on me too. By the time my mother and brother-in-law arrived I decided that I'd better go. Things were getting pretty bad. I told my mother I needed to at least comb my hair; I looked a mess. She was so nervous at this point that she ran out to the car to get Barry to come and help get me out, but he'd have nothing to do with it. She put a hairbrush in my hand and told me to brush my hair in the car. Bill dragged me along as best he could until we were in the back seat of an old 38 Dodge. I could see Barry's face in the rear view mirror. Normally a calm and serene person, I could see the tension on his face, when suddenly a police officer stopped him for speeding in a school zone. Just at that point I let out a scream and the policeman pointing straight ahead, hollered, "Not on my beat." We continued speeding to the hospital. It seemed so far away. I had never heard Barry use any off color language, then looking at his tense face in the mirror I heard him shout, "Where the hell is that place?" Miserable as I felt, I had to smile.

Shortly after that we arrived at the hospital and our driver was so beside himself he drove right past the main entrance to a parking lot a good 100 feet away. Everyone was so distraught. Bill tried to get me out of the car but I couldn't walk. Barry was so distressed He was useless. Bill had to carry me in those strong arms and I had gained so much weight that I was a good 20 pounds heavier than he was. He had to push the heavy hospital door with his body while carrying me in his arms. He made it to the desk and the idiot girl started asking him insurance questions. I let out another shriek. She sent for a nurse and a wheel chair. The nurse brought me up in an elevator giving me a tongue lashing all the way for not coming in sooner. Within minutes I gave birth to a lovely baby girl, while still in my bra and slip.

It has made a great story through the years, but as Bill held me in his arms my mind did a quick rewind to how much I depended on the strength of those arms. How can this be true?

Bill called Rod and got the answering machine. He left a message that we were on our way. We didn't want him worrying about us driving in such a state, so he did not tell him why we were coming. Dr. O'Brien called just after Bill hung up the phone and asked if we had talked to Dr. Candie. He went on trying to encourage me telling me at the end of each sentence that mine was a good tumor. I kept thinking, "How can they call any tumor on the brain a good tumor?" I only knew of two people in my life that had brain tumors, and they were both dead. By the time he said it about four times, I couldn't help myself and I said, "You make me feel like I just won the lottery."

"Oh you're such a nice lady, why did this happen to you?"

My body was beginning to quiet down as Dr. O'Brien made arrangements for us to stop at his office and he would take us to the neuro surgeon, Dr. Case, whose office was in the same building as his. I also requested he call our son Rod and our son Scott and his wife, all doctors, she a neurologist.

"My you have a lot of medical people in your family."

"Yes, and they'll be watching every move you people make."

We both laughed and said good-bye.

I was beginning to calm down a little. As we started putting a few things into an overnight bag the phone started ringing. Scott called. He had just spoken to Dr.O'Brien, and of course he was very upset. Dealing with tragic medical problems every day was one thing, but when it's a family member it becomes something else. He wanted details of how we were handling the situation and suggested we go to the hospital where he practices and have things taken care of there. Bill explained that we were too involved with MGH to make a change at this point and that Rod would be coming to all appointments and advising us on decisions. We just assumed that part, but knowing Rod, we knew that's the way it would be. Brothers and sisters were calling each other and our phone rang so many times it was midnight before we got out of the house. It was a long, tense, two-hour drive. The little talking we did was to support each other. We finally arrived at Rod's house. He and Alice were worried, wondering if we had gotten into an accident. They had called the house several times and only got the answering machine. Dr. O'Brien had talked to Rod. He knew how upset his father must have been driving up. He began to imagine all kinds of things, as a parent does when their children are late coming home at night. No one got much sleep that night and as we anticipated, Rod was ready to go with us in the morning.

Bill, Rod and I sat in Dr. Case's office. He was a handsome man, a blond Clark Gable. Behind him was the MRI negative in front of those lights doctors use to examine them. I was stunned as a cat in front of a snarling dog, sitting there staring at the pictures. Finally I said to the doctor, "Are you sure they're mine?"

All three pair of eyes came at me at once like I had snapped my moorings. Maybe I had. Dr. Case assured me that they were mine. The tumor sat on my brain like a light bulb.

"How can this be when I don't feel sick?"

Then the interrogation began.

"Tell me about the day you passed out in the beauty parlor?" I went through the whole story again for what seemed like the hundredth time. I went on to tell him that I would have been fine if I could have lain down.

"And how often did you get these feelings before you passed out?"

"Well it may have happened several times in the course of the winter, but I would lie on the bed and it only lasted three to five minutes and then I would feel perfect. Not enough to bother thinking of."

He kept pushing for me to explain the feelings, but I found it difficult to describe except to say that I felt as if I would fall down if I didn't lie down.

"Were they like rising feelings coming up in your body?"

"Yes'" I answered laud and clear. "That's a perfect explanation."

That was the first time I had heard it described that way. It was almost a relief to know how to describe those feelings. The doctor went on to explain that those were mild seizures caused by the tumor. Ordinarily nothing would be done about it unless it grew to the point of giving the patient symptoms. He called it a meningeoma. Now it was interfering with my brain and it would have to come out. He explained the whole procedure of how it would be done. He would take out a section of the scull, working down to the tumor. He would push in the sides and gently lift the bottom to see what blood vessels feed the tumor. He would have to disconnect the blood vessels. I imagined it being like an expert disconnecting a bomb. If all that was successful, he would lift the tumor out and to make it brief, put my head back together again. He explained the possibility of the seizures not ending and my being left with deficits, which would be on the left side since my tumor was on the right side. There were no guarantees or anything. He put me on medication to keep me from getting further seizures and explained that I would continue the medication even after the surgery for at least a year and maybe forever depending on how things went. I liked his candidness.

We left his office with an appointment to have the surgery in two weeks. I was told how fortunate I was to have it discovered before the seizures became much worse. Most people with this condition wind up passing out on the streets and being brought into emergency and being treated on an emergency basis. I tried very hard to tell myself that I was fortunate, but on the other hand, yesterday I thought I was going to have fun for the rest of the summer. Life can play some dirty tricks on us.

4

ACCEPTANCE

We drove back to our little place on the Cape and as we entered our condo we both seemed to be looking around like people who had just moved in and found it strange to be there. I suppose it was our way of trying to absorb all that had taken place in the last 20 hours or so. I'm not sure exactly of Bill's feelings but he seemed to be watching every move I made, as if I was going to disappear if he took his eyes off of me. I was in a state of shock, not quite believing what was going on and thinking I would wake up and find it was all only a dream. As the children called and I talked to them, the verbalizing and listening to my own voice made me realize it was real. For the first time since we arrived on the Cape this summer, having fun seemed unimportant. I lost my enthusiasm for the lake and the beach. I did a lot of praying and a lot of thinking. As word of my condition spread, I got calls and cards from friends promising their prayers. Some had put my name on prayer lines and some entered me in spiritual enrollments. I was truly grateful for all their concerns but had to wonder how I could feel so physically well most of the time and still be in danger of it all ending in such a short time. I did have an inner peace that seemed to tell me to get my house in order, "just in case."

I had always been the one that took care of the little annoying things like writing checks for the bills, making sure birthday and Christmas cards were sent, and a million other unnoticeable things. I began wondering if my haphazard way of keeping things in order would even be understandable to Bill. Just in case it were all left to him. He has always been a very meticulous person about all the things he takes care of and when he sees me with my little tiny pieces of paper held together with a paper clip, it drives him crazy. I've been doing things that way all my life and it works for me, but now I began to picture him trying to find receipts or bills or just about anything that my "everything top drawer," contained and going nuts in the process. Just another way we are opposite I guess. I started trying to put things in order. I didn't want Bill to know what I was doing because I didn't want him to think I might be thinking of "checking out." When he would see me writing lists in notebooks and putting things in envelopes and would ask me what I was doing, I felt like the cereal commercial saying, "Nuttin Honey." He had to be thinking, "she lies like a rug."

Bill was being more attentive to me than ever and I'm sure he was as concerned as I was that our days together might not be as long as we expected. I must admit I was enjoying the attention. Sometimes I would even tell myself that this brain surgery might be well worth it. I was not only getting all my own way but whatever I wanted to have or do was perfectly all right with Bill. Was I back on another honeymoon? Strangely, there was nothing in particular that I wanted except to be with him.

Nights were difficult. The medication the doctor gave me to sleep worked fine but I would only sleep two or three hours when I would wake. Bill was not sleeping too well either, so I would try not to stir for fear of disturbing him. Laying in the quiet, dark of night was a setting for deep meditation. My mind traveled through time to all sorts of places and circumstances, but it always came back to the family that I loved and the thoughts of leaving them brought tears to my eyes. My only consolation was to think of the beautiful daughter that had gone before us and that I would perhaps be with her again.

Later that week, Rod called and had set up an appointment with a doctor Coe who was head of the neurology department at MGH. Rod said, "I know you've had it with seeing doctors, but I've done some research and you know Mom that heart problems are very strong on your side of the family, so I just want to be sure that your heart is strong enough to withstand the surgery."

I knew he was going to these extremes because he loved me, so of course we had no choice but to consent to making another trip to Boston. The next evening we arrived at Rod's house and early the next morning the three of us were off to the hospital.

Doctor Coe had a young lady, whom I assume was a resident, interview me before we even met him. Here I go again. The same questions, the same answers. I began to think I should have made a tape and just sent them all a copy. I'm sure if I did that they'd have some reason why they had to observe my facial expressions or something. After a fairly long interrogation, she said the doctor would be with us shortly. We waited, when in came one of MGH's finest. He sat going over the questions and answers with me and added questions about my father's side of the family's heart history. Then he changed the subject and asked me, "How do you happen to know Guy?"

Guy is the friend that Rod made contact with to make this appointment. You don't get overnight appointments with one this high on the upper echelon without a connection.

"My son made the appointment."

He then looked at Rod, I think for the first time. Rod is about five foot nine, medium build with a young and good-looking face. His attire was less than casual.

"Do you work in the same lab with Guy?"

"I used to, but now I have my own lab."

"Then you're a professor at Harvard Medical School?"

The question was asked with a tone of amazement.

"Yes", said Rod in his usual humble way.

They began to carry on a conversation and I sat back getting a big charge out of the new respect the doctor was showing for the young man he barely looked at before.

The final decision on leaving doctor Coe's office was one more test, an electro encephalogram that measures the brain waves. It shows spikes if any heartbeats are abnormal. At least that's the way this lay-man understood it. The test was set up for that afternoon. Rod left us to go to his lab and Bill and I went to a little Lebanese restaurant and had kabobs for lunch. After lunch we went to the building where I was scheduled to have the test. I didn't know where I was most of the time and just followed along like a puppy dog.

This test was another case of being made comfortable and then having the technician put all kinds of wire contraptions all over my head, much like an old fashioned permanent wave, for those old enough to remember. It took quite awhile and I again lay quietly but at least I was not enclosed. Hours later we took the train and eventually were back at Rod's house. We gathered our belongings, kissed Alice good-bye, got into our car and headed for the Cape. The next day we heard from Rod that the test proved positive and he was satisfied that my heart could withstand the surgery. It was on, with only a little more than a week to go.

That night I lay having my middle of the night thoughts. I could feel Bill tossing and turning more than usual. I wanted to slip out of the bed and just sit in the living room, perhaps read to occupy my mind. On one of his tosses, I took advantage of the movement and quietly slipped away. Out in the living room, I picked up a magazine but found I was reading words with my lips but my thoughts were on my family. Closing the magazine I made a decision. I would write a let-ter to each of my loved ones but they would only receive them if I didn't come through the surgery. My thoughts of never saying good-bye are a horrible thought to me. I remember when our second daugh-ter was dying of leukemia at 25 years old, she could not let go until we all individually said good-bye to her and then she was able to pass peacefully on. Now I seemed to understand what she must have felt. Then I'd almost laugh at myself because no one expected me to die, nor did I, but when they open such vital organs as a brain or a heart, you know deep inside that there is always the possibility. So I would have seven letters to write in as many nights. Tonight I would start with our first born, Dennis. He was our adventure child, he left home after college and headed for Alaska where he taught school at Indian villages along the Yukon River and it's tributaries. I sat at the breakfast bar with pen in hand concentrating on that one child. After teaching for 23 years in Alaska he took retirement and left to teach in Africa for the International School System. We've only seen him once in awhile when he visits or vice versa. But we have always been in touch, either by phone or mail. Strangely, shortly after we found out about my problem, the phone rang about one in the morning. Bill jumped out of bed to answer it, thinking something must have been wrong. Who was it but Denny. He had been on safari and reached a place where there was a phone. His Dad told him the bad news and then I got on the phone. Denny had been thinking about us for the past couple of days so when he got a chance to use a phone, he called, apologizing for the hour. No one will ever tell me we don't have some kind of unexplainable bond with our children, or anyone we love dearly. He said he would be calling periodically when he got back to the school, but Bill said to call his sister Kathy, as no one would be at home here. Kathy could keep him informed on exactly how things were going. With all these thoughts in mind, I began my letter with, "My wandering son is off someplace in the universe fulfilling his spirit of adventure. How appropriate that we say our good-byes in writing. Haven't we been keeping each other up on the news with the pen for the past twenty something years?" I went on with a little reminiscing of joys and sorrows in his growing up years. I finished by reinforcing again how much we loved that first born who lived life to the fullest but missed so very much in his own family. When I was satisfied with my letter I put it into an envelope, put his name on it, and hid it under the microwave along with plain papers and envelopes for my next six letters. Now I felt I could fall asleep. I was to have my last visit with doctor Coin the next day.

Donald called first thing in the morning to say that he and Linda would be arriving the next day to spend a couple of days with us. I was delighted. I said to myself, "I must be going to die for Donald to take time off in the middle of the week to visit me." Then I secretly laughed at my thought. Don worked long hours but he was compensated with big bucks. I often think of the second medical school graduation in our family. It was out at University of Massachusetts Medical School and I wanted a duplicate of the picture taken at Rod's graduation only with Scott in the middle. In my pride I was saying, "Imagine two doctors!" Don, our baby, might have been a little upset with me being so proud of his brothers, then I heard him say in a kind of low resentful voice, "I'll buy and sell the both of them." He later graduated from the Harvard Business School and works like a Trojan. At this point I think he could buy and sell the whole family. These are the joys of a large family; they're all so different.

We kept the appointment with Doctor Coin in the afternoon, although a broken leg seemed insignificant at this point. Doctor Coin thought the leg looked good and I told him I had taken the cast off at the six-week date and it felt fine. He was glad it turned out fine and said this would be the last visit. I answered that it had better be because next Tuesday I had to have brain surgery. The look on his face was priceless as his head and eyes popped like a grasshopper from my leg to my face. "What is the problem?" he asked. I explained how a meningeoma was found on my brain and it had to be removed. He was obviously sympathetic and wished me luck. I'm not sure if that was encouraging or discouraging. I told Bill on the way home how I had told the doctor about my taking the cast off at the six-week date. It was obvious that Bill could care less at this point. The day went on like a flowing river. More cards arrived, people called, including Pam, who was going to tell all the high school committee why I couldn't be at the meeting. She offered to take me anywhere that I might need a ride since I was not allowed to drive. The doctor said I would not be able to drive until I had gone six months without seizures. That I found to be a big loss. Bill and I were getting like Siamese twins. It was both wonderful and awful. We're bound to get sick of each other I would think.

The next day we waited for Don and his wife to arrive. Next to Denny we saw the least of him and I never wanted it to get as seldom as we saw Denny. Bill would often say to me, "If only I hadn't allowed him to go to Alaska." He was referring to Denny's junior year in college. It was in the sixties when all the Vietnam protesting was going on and colleges shut down early in the spring because so many administration buildings had been taken over by students protesting the Vietnam War. It had not happened at Boston College but along with many other schools they chose to shut down early. Denny came home while school was still going on and told me he intended to ask his father at supper if he could go to Alaska for the summer. He knew a kid who claimed he had "air hitched" to Alaska the previous summer and filled Denny's head with all kinds of adventuresome things. I thought it was a bad idea. I could picture Bill blowing the roof off the house, but my thoughts meant little to Denny. His younger sisters listened to Denny and I discussing it while dinner was being prepared. The dinner table was unusually quiet that night, all of us dreading the big question that was to come up. Denny must have been giving it a little thought too as it was at least dessert time before the subject came up. He prefaced it with, "You know Dad that college is closing early this spring."

"I read the papers," his father said.

"Well, I was thinking I'd like to air-hitch to Alaska."

Then he went on with a long story about his friend who claimed he had done it—Silence—Except for Donald banging a spoon on his high chair tray. Bill was in deep thought and the other kids felt like getting out of there but they stayed and listened as their father finally opened his mouth.

"You know son, if I was a young man I think I'd join you."

We all reacted with a sigh of relief and shock. I knew Bill made that decision because of the times. He was a World War 2 veteran and we grew up in the generation when if our government said something was right, we didn't question them. He did not want his son protesting. Now Bill blames himself because Dennis is always gone, but I believe that Denny could never have been kept down. He's just an adventurer and would have found his adventure one way or another.

Today Don was going to be with us, and that was good. He planned on leaving immediately after work, but with a five-hour drive from New York, they wouldn't arrive until 10 or 11 at night. He would take the next day off of work and leave sometime in the late afternoon to get back late that night. Whenever Don visited it was never for much more than 36 hours, but we were happy for whatever time he could squeeze into his busy schedule.

They arrived near mid-night, both were tired and ready to go to bed. I told him they could take the large room with the twin beds and then remembering that they are married less than a year, I added, "You can push the beds together if you want to."

Bill didn't hear me saying that and when they put their bags in the room, the two of them went immediately to the outsides of the beds and started pushing them together. We were still in the hall watching and I was thinking, "Ah! Newly weds, isn't it wonderful?"

We all kissed each other good night and Bill and I went into our bedroom. No sooner had we shut the door and he doubled up laughing. He said, "I couldn't believe it when the first thing they did was push the beds together."

Then I told him that I said they could do that if they wanted to, but to tell the truth I didn't think they'd do it right in front of us. How could I think that way? Donald always said and did exactly what he was thinking. You knew where you stood with Don.

The next day it felt great to have young people in the house again. They were up early and out jogging before we even got started for breakfast. We talked, we laughed and just enjoyed each other and all too soon the day was gone and it was time for them to leave. As we were saying good-bye, Don said, "I'm flying from New York early Tuesday morning Mom, I'll be at the hospital with Dad."

Just as he was getting into his car he repeated, "Don't forget, I'll be in the hospital on Tuesday."

I smiled and shook my head as if to say yes. They drove away. I thought to myself, "*Good God, Donald's taking two days off work! This is serious stuff.*"

When I was able to sneak out of bed during my wake time that night, I had to write two of my letters. With Don and Linda in the house the night before, I was afraid someone may catch me up, so I just lay quietly in bed for a few hours, thinking and praying until I fell back to sleep. This night I would write my letters to Kathy and Rod. In Kathy's letter I mention how tired she must be about hearing the story of her birth because it has made such a great story for so many years. I told her how much she has made up for being the cholicy baby that she was for seven months. I thanked her for giving us three lovely grand daughters and for being the glue that makes the siblings stick together, the many celebration parties we've held at her house since we began living condo style. There were hundreds of things I wanted to say to her, but I kept the letter brief, expressing our love and thanks for having such a great daughter. As I finished that letter, Bill called from the bedroom, "Where are you?"

I shuffled all my papers under the microwave in case he got up. I grabbed a magazine.

"I'm just reading for awhile until I get sleepy."

He was standing at the kitchen door by the time I finished my sentence.

"Are you all right?"

"I'm fine. I just woke up, wide awake and thought a little reading would make me sleepy, you go on back to bed."

"O.K. but call me if you need me for anything."

"I'll be in shortly."

I hoped he would just go in and go back to sleep so I could finish what I set out to do. He left and I waited awhile until I thought he must have gone back to sleep before I pulled my papers out from under the microwave. It was time to think of Rod. I thought of where he fell in the family. There were three older and three younger than he and it made me think of a poem I had learned as a little girl. It was about the oldest child being given attention and responsibilities and the youngest being pampered and spoiled. The only line I remember in the poem is, "but I'm the middle child." Well Rod was surely the middle child, having three on each side of him. I wondered if I could possibly express to him what a joy he had been in the family, but I tried. I thanked him for being the wonderful son that he is and asked him to always spread that love to his brothers and sisters because love is very contagious. I had three letters done and four to go.

The next day was Friday and that was the day the decision was made that Bill would not be coming back here to the Cape while I was in the hospital. Instead he would stay at my sister's house because she lives a short walk to a subway station where he could take public transportation right to the hospital. That was easier than driving into Boston. In view of that decision, I decided to organize the food in the refrigerator. I have a real fetish about wasting food that drives Bill crazy, but as I said before, since the tumor was discovered, I could do no wrong. I packaged the leftovers we would not be eating immediately and put them in the freezer. I would give everything a final check just before leaving for the hospital.

The phone rang. Scott and Susanne and the two children would be coming by tomorrow, just for the day. I knew Bill was thinking, as I was that it would keep ours minds off the upcoming surgery at least for a day. We went out for a few hours in the afternoon. Before we knew it the day was over. One day closer.

This would be my night to write to Mary. Mary was the fifth child in the family and the third girl. For the first time I had trouble during a pregnancy, but not until the sixth month. As a result Mary was very premature. She was born about eleven weeks too soon. Back in 1955 preemies were put in isolation and fed through tubes. It was a transparent plastic box where we could look at her but she was never touched. There were two holes about six inches in diameter on each side, where a nurse could reach in to change her diaper. She was to be kept there until her weight increased to four and a half or five pounds. After leaving the hospital we would visit every few days to see how she was progressing. It was almost two months before we could bring her home. Even then she seemed so small. With all my experience with babies, I was still nervous handling her. She grew very slowly and seemed to have difficulty responding to stimuli. It took a good two years for her to begin to respond to the rest of the family trying to play with her and we constantly worried whether she would ever progress. All we got from doctors was "wait and see." It was very frustrating. She did improve but always had emotional problems and difficulties relating to children outside the family. She was always under the care of Pediatricians, Neurologists and any doctor we thought could help her. Growing up I would bring her to therapy once a week. She required a great deal of attention. Fortunately, she got a lot of that from older brothers and especially from her two older sisters. Of course it is well known today that babies should be touched and held from the time of birth and I continue to look back on that bad start as the beginnings of her problems. She had a severe breakdown at the age of sixteen. That is a whole other story, but to get back to my thoughts this night, I had to recall the past. Now Mary has found a man who loves her and she even has a little girl of her own. She is on permanent medication and at times has set backs, she understands her problems and is dealing with them. With all this in mind, I started my letter. "Dear Mary; You have always been our special child since the day you were born, so tiny and so much earlier than you were expected." I went on to tell her that I understood how difficult it was for her growing up, but how she had persevered. Now she was married with a beautiful little girl that she named after her deceased sister who she loved very much. I told her of how proud we are of how much she has overcome and what a great job she is doing of raising our lovely grand daughter. I reminded her of all the prayers and watching over she will continue to receive from her sister in heaven and I added from me, knowing she will never see this if everything is successful.

Scott and Susanne arrived in the morning with our two youngest grand children. Scott and Denny are similar in looks. Tall, dark and handsome my sister would tell me. Perhaps I'm prejudiced, but I agreed. He certainly looked that way as he lifted his little girl up on his broad shoulders. Susanne, slender with dark classic features, took their son by the hand. They were a beautiful sight as they walked toward the house. They're two are the only babies left so far in the family. There is a good ten or twelve years between the next youngest and Scott's children. When the family manages to get together, Scott and Susanne have built in baby sitters; the cousins vary so much in age. We enjoy these little ones so much when we see them. At one and three years old, they are so full of energy I keep thinking that if we could bottle it and save it for later in life it would be great, but such is not the case. Scott presented me with a big bag of tomatoes from his garden. He used to have a garden when he was in high school and the family enjoyed the fruits of his labors. I missed the wonderful tomatoes when Scott was gone from the nest and he knew it. I remembered one day when I got home from teaching school and went into the dining room to see a place set at the table with a luscious looking salad and a bottle of wine and wine glass. I went over to the setting and there was a note that went something like this.

"Dear Mom; Enjoy! Love Scott."

I was more touched than he could ever know. He had gotten home before me and I'm sure he stuffed his face as he always did after school, including a salad with his garden vegetables so he made one for me too and went on his way to whatever; Probably fishing, his favorite after school sport. When I went to get the dressing for the salad I discovered we were out of it, and I thought, "that little devil." I ate it anyway. I would think of that each time he brought me tomatoes.

We spent the morning at home and after lunch we went to the lake. We ended the afternoon with ice cream from Smugglers, a little ice cream shop only a short walk from our place. They didn't want to leave too late so after we all had ice cream it was time for them to hit the road and try to avoid some of the late traffic.

Bill and I went to church that night instead of going the next morning. We were early for the Mass and I noticed a light on in one of the confessionals near where we were sitting. I decided I was getting prepared for anything that might happen to me, so I'd better prepare spiritually too. I told Bill I was going to confession as I left the pew where we were sitting. As I knelt in the confessional box, for the first time I felt my eyes well up with tears. When the priest opened the slider to my side of the box, I felt so emotional I could hardly talk. I managed to tell him I was going to have brain surgery on Tuesday and wanted to be prepared. He was just wonderful, giving me absolution for all the sins of my life and promising his prayers and offering his Mass on that day for me. I knew I would be all ready as soon as I finished my letters.

How appropriate that I had spent that day with Scott since this was the night I intended to write my letter to him. Scott was such a sweet baby, lovable and responsive from the very beginning. I told him that in the letter and went on to say, "I sometimes worried that I might short change you and Donald because of you growing in the shadow of a child that required so much attention. I tried very hard not to let that happen. I called you sweet Scott because you demanded so little, but quietly grew like a flower, happy to go fishing or work in your garden. You had your hectic moments, investigating things you shouldn't be into, but they were few and far between." I wrote of his lovely wife and children and asked him to continue calling his Dad often and visiting him, as I knew how much Bill enjoyed seeing his little grand children. Towards the end of the letter I said, "Now you have children of your own and you know how much a parent loves their children. It doesn't change because they grow up." I reinforced my love for him and reminded him that one day we would all be together again. Then I went back to bed, peaceful that I was almost ready.

On Sunday we got some of our things together that we were going to take with us. I gathered my cards and notes that I had received from friends and put them into a basket. In the afternoon we went out for a little drive, ending with an ice cream from Smuggler's. We spent the evening just watching T.V. interrupted periodically with phone calls asking how I was doing. Sometimes I felt they should be asking how Bill was doing. I decided it was harder on him, as I was pretty well accepting however it may turn out and he had to worry about just that. At this point I wouldn't swap places with him. We finally went to bed about eleven thirty, after the news.

I woke as usual about two in the morning and slipped quietly out of bed to complete my work. I got all my papers out from under the microwave and focused my thoughts on Donald. I sat for ten or fifteen minutes just thinking of him from the time he was a baby. Now I was ready to write.

"Dear Donald; Our baby. I know you don't like to be called that but you will always be our baby. It couldn't have hurt, for you were always full of confidence. Remember how you'd tell me that I saved the best for last? How I enjoyed watching you and Scott grow up. From experience I knew some of the annoying things were just stages, so you guys got away with a lot more than your older brothers and sisters. I remember when you were only thirteen or fourteen and you gave me a two-minute soliloquy on the plans for your life. I got such a kick out of it, but I just smiled and said, "Good luck kid." I must admit that you pretty much have stuck to that plan and by the grace of God and a lot of hard work from you, things have worked out pretty well for you." I continued by reminding him that sometimes life throws us a curve and it upsets the best of plans. I knew that if and when that should happen he would have the fortitude to handle it well. I reminisced about some of the major events in his life both good and bad and told him how much I enjoyed getting to know Linda a little better on his trip here last week. Of course I told him again how much he is loved and to stay close to his family. I know they will always be supportive of each other and I would always be with him in spirit.

It was now close to three thirty in the morning and I was still wide-awake. I assessed all I had accomplished up until now and thought to myself that as long as I was so awake I should write my good-bye letter to Bill. I thought I really had nothing to say to Bill since we already knew so much about each other. I was confident of his love and I thought he must feel the same about me, but much to my surprise when I began to write I found myself going on and on. His was the longest letter of all. Some of it was my usual nagging not to take life so seriously and to laugh more over trivial things. I reviewed the fact that we had survived through many mountains and valleys together. I told him I loved him even when we couldn't stand each other for our differences. We lived our lives to the fullest and now I wanted him to continue doing the same. I ended by saying, "I'll always be with you. Make me happy by being happy yourself. I love you always." I put all seven envelopes into a large brown envelope and put that into one of my drawers. I was ready. Tomorrow we would go to my sister's house and the next morning we would be off for surgery.

5

THE BIG DAY

I didn't get much sleep the previous night but there were things to be done on this my last day at home. I wanted to leave everything in good shape not knowing what the future held for me. I started cleaning the house but Bill kept insisting I not do it, that he would take care of it. He thought the place looked fine anyway and he wanted to talk to me. We sat down to have a few serious words. He wanted to know if I wanted to recuperate at one of the children's houses or my sister's house or come home. It never even occurred to me to be any place but home. I think he was glad to hear that. He said what he'd like to do is open the sofa bed in the living room and kind of turn it into a bedroom so that he could take care of me close to the kitchen and I could sleep or watch TV. *There he wants to be prepared for everything again*, I thought but I didn't say it, I just said that it would be fine by me. He finished all the cleaning and after lunch we put together the rest of the things we would need in the next week. I checked everything in the refrigerator, putting things in the freezer. Then I saw the beautiful tomatoes Scott had brought and decided to take them with me. I'd give some to my sister and bring the rest for Alice and Alice will be able to split with the others.

"I don't think you should do that. You're going in for brain surgery and you're worried about tomatoes! I'll never understand you."

"You know I can't waste them and they'd be rotten by the time we got home."

If a look can have both love and disgust in it, that was the look I got. So I continued getting things in order. Just as we were about to leave I told Bill that there was a large brown envelope in the drawer with my underwear and he was to open it only if anything went wrong and I did not come out of the surgery. He looked at me with an astonished expression, so I continued to explain that I just wrote a few words to the kids in the event that I died.

"Don't say that," he said.

"Of course I'll be fine, but just in case, O.K.?"

"Yes" he answered. Then we got on the road early enough to stop for supper and arrive at my sister's in the early evening. Things worked as planned and Marion was so happy we were there. She had a doctor's appointment the next afternoon at Mass General. I told her I had to be at the hospital at 7 in the morning for a final CAT scan. The doctor had said he wanted that just before the surgery in order to pin point exactly where to cut. The surgery was scheduled for 11 AM. Her husband, Barry, insisted on driving us to the hospital in the morning.

After a restless night we were up bright and early to shower and dress. I was feeling calm and peaceful as I took my tomatoes from the refrigerator leaving some for my sister. At 6:30 Barry, Bill and I left the house. The ride was quite uneventful considering that we were the same trio that took a ride to the hospital some forty something years ago for a baby delivery, but no one mentioned it. Barry was so used to this ride that he knew all the back streets to take. Marion had been quite sickly for many years and her doctor was also at MGH. Arriving in about 20 minutes, we thanked him, he wished me luck and we were on our way to the CAT scan area. We logged in at the desk and took a seat in a huge waiting area. After only a short time, Rod, looking rather disheveled and Alice arrived. I said, "you didn't have to get here so early, the surgery isn't until 11."

"We wanted to be here mom."

I thought to myself, *I could always depend on you.* I handed Alice the bag of tomatoes.

"They're right from Scott's garden Alice, you'll love them. You can give some of them to Kathy."

Alice took the bag laughing while the two men gave me that "you're nuts" look.

"Ma you're going in for brain surgery."

I cut him off. "I know, I already heard it from your father."

The clock was ticking and I wasn't getting called for the scan. Rod took things into his own hands, going up to the desk and asking what the problem was. The girl at the desk said something about the doctor's orders not specifying exactly where he wanted the scan and they were waiting to hear. We sat for another 20 minutes or more. Then Rod got up and went to an "in house" telephone and called directly to Dr. Case's office. His secretary said that the doctor just wanted a head scan. Rod stretched the phone cord to have it repeated to the girl at the desk. Within minutes I was called in with all kinds of apologies. I repeat, at the MGH, the medicine is great but the administrative part leaves much to be desired. The scan was easy as I was only partially in the tube. It was over in about 5 minutes. It was about 10 o'clock by that time and the four of us, Alice carrying the tomatoes, headed for the designated area where I would be prepped for the surgery. The family could stay with me until it was time to bring me to the operating room. Then they were to go to another part of the hospital quite a distance away and wait until the doctor called on an "in house phone" to let them know the results of the operation. Bill, Rod, Alice and I talked until the gurney I was on was pushed through those intimidating swinging doors. When that time came they each kissed me and said they would be praying. I could feel the apprehension in each of them, but it did not rub off on me. I was as calm and peaceful as if I had just kissed them good night and was going to my room.

I was pushed down a corridor with rooms on both sides to a specific operating room. Dr. case stopped by and said, "We're finishing cleaning up this next room and then we'll be ready for you. How are you doing?"

"Fine," I said, looking around as best I could from my position. Everyone was in scrubs and masks except me. An anesthesiologist came to me and told me everything she was about to do, "I'm just going to put a line in your arm. Just a little prick. It won't hurt."

And it didn't. Next someone came and started to cut a quadrant of my hair from the front right side and then shave the short hairs. I knew now it was really happening. I had a large bald area, but my body continued to feel calm. Maybe that line she had put in my arm helped with that, I don't know. The nurse saw me looking at a huge something, I didn't know what it was and she said, "Don't let it scare you. It's a large microscope and it will take three people to move it, it's so heavy."

My last thought was that it must be going to be used to look in my brain, and then I fell asleep.

In the meantime, or as the saying goes, meanwhile back at the ranch, Bill, Rod, and Alice were in a large waiting room. Other people were there too, all intently waiting for the volunteer in a small-attached room to call them to the phone. Kathy and her husband George arrived with a large bag of chicken sandwiches, enough for the whole family. One by one the children entered the room and joined their brothers and sisters. The last to arrive was the youngest, Donald. He flew in from New York just as he said he would. With tearful eyes he walked up to his father and said, "Dad, what can I do?"

Bill, appreciating his feelings, just said, "Sit down and pray." Time dragged. Our oldest granddaughter took time from her work to come into the hospital too. They had quite a group. Alice told Kathy to take some of the tomatoes. Like a cloud that was blocking the sun then moved to let the brightness shine, they all had a good laugh about the tomatoes that were getting mushy from being lugged around so much. That got them talking about their mother and some of her strange ways. Donald said, "Remember how mom always said, 'I need that like I need a hole in the head' and now she has one."

The tension was abated as they laughed, talked and remembered. After a couple of hours they opened the sandwiches Kathy had brought and all had some lunch. Others in the waiting room who were watching were wishing they had done the same, but Kathy knew about wait-ing in hospitals from years before when her sister was dying of leukemia. Our physical functions remain the same regardless of what other things are going on in our lives; we still have to eat. She had thought ahead so that no one would have to leave to go to the cafeteria. Each time the phone rang everyone was silent wondering which one was lucky enough to get the call and hear the results of some loved ones surgery. Time drags as watching water boil, so they passed it sometimes in silence and sometimes reminiscing with each other. It was late after-noon before the call came. Bill told Rod to talk to the doctor and so he did. The words flowed from Rod's mouth, "She's all right we can see her soon Dad."

The doctor told him it had gone as well as he had hoped it would and the tumor popped right out. He referred to it as a "magnificent tumor." Relief was the reaction of all the family and Bill gathered them all around him in a circle to say a prayer of thanksgiving.

About that time Barry arrived at the waiting room with my sister in a wheel chair, outside of the immediate family they were the first to hear the good news. Marion would call my other sisters when she got home. I had a good many fans rooting for me; all had to be notified.

At this time someone was shaking my shoulder and saying

"Wake up Helen, wake up. It's over, your surgery is over." Slowly my eyes opened and I had to take time to focus. She repeated her mes-sage to me and then started the neurological stuff.

"Do you know where you are?"

"Yes, I'm in the hospital."

"What is your name?"

"Helen."

"Do you know who the president is?"

I had to think a little, but answered correctly.

"And what year is it?"

Again I had to think but answered correctly.

"Good."

As soon as she stopped talking to me I fell back to sleep. When I opened my eyes again, there was Bill.

"Did Alice give Kathy some of the tomatoes?"

Already I upset him.

"Never mind the tomatoes, how are you doing?"

"I think I'm O.K. I answered all their questions and I think I got an A."

"Are you in much pain?"

"Not yet, I guess I'm still pretty medicated."

"You're something," he bent over and kissed me. "I'm going to let Rod and Alice in now and I'll see you when they move you to your room, only two at a time can come in here."

Each of them visited me for just a few minutes. They all looked so beautiful to me and I thought again of how much I loved them. I guess I went back to sleep. I don't know how many more hours went by but I later learned that the hospital was having trouble finding an available room to put me in. A whole floor in a large hospital dedicated to neurological patients and all beds are full. How is it I only knew two people that had brain tumors? How one bed in a semi private room became available, I don't know, but I eventually wound up in it. The family had maintained their vigilance and was there to greet me. Everyone shocked that I could talk with him or her. All had expected me to be out like a light, but not even brain surgery managed to shut me up, but this time I think they were all happy to hear my voice and listened intently. I've been trying to figure out ever since how I could hold their attention like that again. I loved listening to them laugh and talk together. Donald had to catch a plane to get back to work in the morning so he was the first to kiss me good-bye. Just before leaving he said, "You know mom, you have a good looking head, why don't you have all the rest of your hair shaved off and then it will grow in evenly."

He was serious. I smiled.

Scott had a long drive in front of him and he kissed me and left. About fifteen minutes later a woman came into the room carrying a vase with the most beautiful roses any of us had ever seen. Everyone, even the people visiting my roommate were aghast at the beauty of them. The woman said they were for me from my son. I said, "which one, I have four sons?" she handed me the card and all remaining family were laughing and said it has to be Scott. He got them on his way out. Sure enough it was from "my son." We all admired the gorgeous flowers and laughed at Scott thinking of himself as my only son. I hoped that they all felt special like that. Each in turn said good night and named a time they would be able to get back to see me. Bill stayed and just sat with me. I was so tired after all that excitement, I think I slept most of the time he was there except when a nurse would wake me for medication or whatever.

When I woke it was dark and quiet. I had no idea of the time. Bill had left. I felt terrible, worse than I did right after the surgery. Those rising feelings were back in full force. I rang for the nurse and when she came in I told her how awful I felt. She said she would take care of it after she spoke with the doctor about increasing the medication, which was being fed to me intravenously. After what seemed like a long time and the medication being increased, I finally fell back to sleep. It was a long night.

6

FLOWERS

About 10:30 or 11 the next morning, Bill arrived and I was so happy to see him. He said he spent a good part of the morning answering phone calls from people asking about me. He was a little upset that I didn't seem as well as I had the day before. My answer was that the medication from the surgery was probably still in effect so it fooled me into thinking I was fine. Now I was getting the real aftermath.

The girl in the room with me had about three nice bouquets of flowers spread along the windowsill, which made the room look cheerful. A delivery person arrived at the door calling my name. Bill said, "Right here".

The boy set down two flower arrangements. Bill handed the cards to me. One was from Kathy and one from Dennis. Dennis had no doubt called Kathy and had her send flowers from him. I was sure he didn't send them from Africa, but it pleased me very much. This cheered me up enough to stop thinking about how awful I felt, at least for a while. After only a few moments of pleasant thoughts, in came a large tray of food. Was it lunchtime already? Soup, fruit, a cheeseburger, milk and some kind of desert all looked sickening to me.

"You have to eat to get your strength back."

"I can't" I kept saying, "It makes me sick to look at it. You eat it because I can't eat a single bite."

"I'll go down to the cafeteria for a bite."

"Don't be crazy, it'll only go to waste. You know how I hate that."

When he finally realized I had no intention of touching it, he condescended to eat the cheeseburger. The nurse came in and seeing him, she just laughed. I guess they're used to seeing such things. Then she said to Bill, "You can walk her up the hall if you'd like".

He was shocked, but said "O.K. I will."

He helped me out of the bed, first to a sitting position and then let my legs dangle until he got me into a standing position. He dragged the I.V. pole along with one hand as I leaned on his other side to try to take a few steps. After the first few steps it didn't seem so bad and we slowly walked up the hall toward a solarium where I could sit and rest. A few other people were sitting around too. One man sitting there began talking to me. He told me he had a brain tumor that turned out to be malignant and he was scheduled for all kinds of radiation appointments. As we walked slowly back to my room I looked into rooms that we passed and could see people of all ages who looked to be in various stages of illness and my heart went out to them as I thanked God for my *"good" tumor*.

Alice came in late in the afternoon. Rod had to take a trip that day to give a paper or something but she said he would be in the next day. She brought a box of Chinese pastries that looked so good but I still couldn't eat any. She said, "Maybe tomorrow you'll feel like them".

The afternoon passed and more food was brought in for supper. I kept trying to fluff it off on whoever was around, but I was not about to try any myself. I just kept hanging on to my diaphragm. That evening another pretty basket of flowers arrived for me. I was thrilled as I read the card. It was from my high school friends of 50 years ago. I felt so nostalgic; I know my eyes filled with tears as I showed the card to the ones in the room. I couldn't make the reunion plans but by golly I'd get to go to it.

I slept better that night, waking only about twice to request pain medication for my headache. However in the morning when I moved about the bed the rising feelings were still with me, but not quite as strong as they were the day before. This at least gave me hope that they would eventually go away. I ate no breakfast again. Bill arrived in the middle of the morning and so did the husband of my roommate. Bill and he got talking to each other mostly about having a wife that took seizures. Her husband had been living with the situation for so long that he handled it in stride, but that was the first time I realized that Bill was in mortal fear that I would take a seizure at any time. Then I remembered that on one of my doctor visits Bill asking the doctor if I could become epileptic and the doctor said it was possible. Bill asked him what he would do if I passed out on the street. The doctor said that he should get me immediately to a hospital. As he talked to the other husband I knew how much he must worry about that happening. I nearly died as her husband began explaining to Bill how to hold the head, etc. in the event of a seizure. Of course I had no intention of that happening to me, but Bill was not about to listen if I tried saying that to him. For the first time I was glad to see food being brought in to disrupt this conversation. Food still turned me off, but it was better than listening to How to Deal with A Seizure 101 class. I drank a little of the liquids as Bill ate some of the food. In the afternoon we again went for a little walk. When we got back to the room there was another large flower arrangement that Donald had sent. It was very beautiful, but we were beginning to have trouble finding places to put all the flowers. I asked my roommate if it would be all right to put some on the windowsill with hers where we could both enjoy them. No problem. I'm not sure if our room looked more beautiful or like a funeral parlor. We cornered the market on flowers. Before the day was over a couple more arrangements came from friends. Alice and Rod arrived late in the day and there first reaction was "WOW, look at those flowers, but nothing beats those roses". Kathy and George came in shortly after them. I lay back listening to all of them talking with each other and enjoying their comradeship and hanging onto my diaphragm. At one point my grand daughter asked who had sent all the flowers and I started pointing to each bouquet and telling her who the sender was. As I named family members Rod piped up with, "Oh sure, every one in the family sent flowers but me. Make me feel bad."

He said it in his cute sarcastic voice. We laughed so hard at his expression that it hurt my already hurting stomach. Most of them took a little break and went to the cafeteria for coffee. I don't think some of them had supper. My oldest grand daughter stayed with me so I took that opportunity to ask her how she liked the tomatoes. She laughed and told me exactly what happened. She said it was an on going joke about who would hold the tomatoes and they all had a discussion standing outside the recovery room that only I would remember to pack tomatoes on the morning of my surgery. She had me laughing at myself at this point.

"Wait! There was more. Over the day, traveling around the hospital and being held by various people, the tomatoes were getting a bit crushed. In fact they started leaking all over the floor and Donald's shoes at some point outside the recovery room. Dad had to explore the hallways to find a bathroom with paper towels to dry the floor and shoes. I can't remember who took the tomatoes home, or if they were discarded at the hospital, but the next morning when I visited you after your room was changed, Uncle Scott came in and he said he brought more tomatoes for you because he knew how much you love them. All of us exchanged glances and wouldn't let him give them to you. I don't know who wound up getting your tomatoes, Nana."

I laughed my head off, she really made me forget my troubles and when the rest of them came back from the cafeteria I never let on I knew.

Just as everyone was leaving, Mary came in with her husband and daughter. She presented me with a statue, of all things, so here I was in a room loaded with flowers and a statue. I felt like my roommate and I could open a shop. That was the plus side of all this misery, having so much support.

Sleep was intermittent that night and I woke to a new day. It was only Thursday but so much had happened it seemed as if I had been in that hospital for at least a week. I did not however feel like I wanted to go home yet. I went through the usual morning blood drawings, temperature taking, questions, etc. When breakfast was brought in I tried to eat a little of it. Frankly, I felt pretty rotten, but I chatted with my room mate and just doing that was a constant reminder that I would at least get well, at least I thought I would. Bill, Rod and Alice came in the late morning and shortly after that the surgeon arrived. He checked my stitches, asked a lot of questions then, much to everyone's surprise, said, "I think you can go home on Saturday."

This was such a shock to me I didn't feel ready. He added, "The stitches can come out in a week, you don't have to come into Boston, and any doctor can do it."

"How about if I have Rod take them out I said".

"That'll be fine."

As he was about to leave the room, Rod said, "Oh doctor, while you had her head open were you able to get out any of that guilt chip?"

"No, that Catholic guilt chip is in too deep to take out."

We all had a good laugh until the realization that I would be leaving the hospital in only two days finally sunk in. Bill said, "I hope you're not going to ask to go to Lisa's shower!"

In all sincerity I answered, "No, I know I wouldn't be up to it."

Bill was both relieved and worried, that wasn't like me. Then Rod, who had been doing medical research for the past ten years, said, "Mom, how could you trust your head to me? You know I haven't touched a patient for ten years."

"There's no one I'd rather trust my head to."

And I meant that. So we had a date for Rod to come to our house next Tuesday and take out my stitches.

The day felt very long to me. I couldn't seem to be able to take a nap. It seemed as if people were coming and going all day long. Two of my sisters came for a short visit in the evening bringing me more gifts. They were really surprised when they heard how soon I was getting out of the hospital. We talked about the days when you spent longer in the hospital after having a baby then you do today after brain surgery.

I slept pretty well that night and when the aid came in to change the bed I offered to get up and sit in the chair to make the job easier for her. She was grateful for that and helped me out of the bed and into the chair. Those risings were attacking me but I was getting used to that happening in the morning and said nothing. Suddenly I opened me eyes with everyone watching me. De JA Vu I was back in the beauty parlor.

"What happened?"

"You had a seizure."

"Well what do we do about it?"

"The doctor has been notified."

Oh great, I was thinking, I thought I was through with that stuff, as they helped me back into the bed. The result was more monitoring of medication, maybe an increase, I don't really know. When Bill came in the late morning, I began to tell him, but he already knew about it. My going home date got extended to Sunday, for which I was glad. I think my thoughts were beginning to be like Bill's. What was going to happen? The doctor came in a little later in the day and was very casual about my taking a seizure, except to explain that they would keep me an extra day to monitor me. He walked to my bedside and said, "I'm going to remove the bandage today."

I was preparing myself for a very dramatic experience, like something you'd see in the movies. I hadn't seen myself in a mirror and imagined that my head was well bandaged. Then I heard a zap and he said the bandage was off. I guess I was disappointed. My dramatic moments never seemed to be dramatic. Apparently the bandage was taped only over the incision and the rest of my head was just bald on that side. No wonder the kids were telling me I had a nice head. I didn't realize so much of it showed.

Friday and Saturday were much of the same, monitoring medicines, checking Dilantin blood levels, taking a walk to the solarium with Bill.

My kids all visited. I tried choking down a little food. I talked with my roommate, who was beginning to run a fever postponing her surgery. I didn't feel particularly happy and yet I knew I had no right to feel that way, so I pretended as best I could. Sunday arrived, the going home day. My doctor came in to officially discharge me and told me he was going away the following week but named the doctor who would be covering for him and I should call him if I had any problems. This made me feel even more apprehensive but I said nothing about that. About noontime I left the hospital with Bill armed with prescriptions and all the instructions I supposedly would need. Once I was in the car, it felt good to be outside. I thought of all the family who would be at Lisa's wedding shower, but I knew that I would at least get to the wedding that was about two months away. The weather was nice with still a little summer heat in the air but fall only a breath away. I always loved fall in New England so I knew we would spend our time quietly going from day to day.

When we arrived back at the house it felt good to be there. I felt as if I had been away for a long time. Time has a way of being mysterious. Sometimes it seems to drag and other times it seems to pass almost too quickly. I guess that's one of life's mysteries. I rested on the bed while Bill pulled out the sofa bed in the living room and made up the bed. When he got me all settled in, he asked if I'd be well enough to leave alone long enough for him to do a little grocery shopping. I was perfectly comfortable and felt fine. I had to promise not to get up or try to do anything while he was gone. I promised, knowing he'd be a wreck leaving me if I didn't. He was back in about an hour and began making some supper for us but he knew I couldn't eat much.

After that we settled back to watch some TV for the evening and I began to feel comfortable and cherished. It was good to be home.

7

PAMPERED

Changing the living room into a bedroom was definitely a good idea. Everything to make life comfortable was within reach. The telephone, the television, the kitchen, the bathroom were all only a few steps away. Bill started out doing every little thing that needed to be done on our first full day at home. In the afternoon Alice came in with a couple of baskets of flowers I had asked her to bring from the hospital. I knew it would drive Bill nuts if I started picking up baskets when we were leaving. He looked at me and said, "You told her to do that didn't you?" Alice and I both laughed. Just about that time the doorbell rang and it was a florist delivering a basket of plants from one of our friends. "Are we going to have this place looking like a florist shop too?" Bill said. "Wouldn't that be nice," I answered sarcastically. Other than little things like that, I could do no wrong, at least for a while. Alice said Rod and she would be over the next day so he could remove the stitches. I was looking forward to it. In the mail that day came a package for me. When I opened it I found a very pretty crushable straw hat in white with a large brim. It was from Scott and his wife. She, being a neurologist, was familiar with patients who had to have their hair shaved off. The hat was the perfect gift. With it on I looked pretty good and who would ever know what was underneath. Alice had left a big plate of goodies she had brought from the shower I missed. My appetite was improving when I didn't have that nauseous feeling, which wasn't too often, so I sat with my hat on eating nice fattening things. Bill was happy for those normal moments and I was too. We spent a quiet evening watching TV with Bill bringing me my medicine as the doctor had directed and making meals that I was willing to try eating. Whenever I was tired I would doze off to sleep and all seemed to be going along just fine. Bill slept with me that night in the sofa bed and after a week apart it felt good to have his body next to mine, but I always had to have my back to him because he always slept on my right and I could only lay my head on the left side. That was all right at least we were together again.

The next day was exciting for me as our son was coming to remove the stitches from my head. This not only meant I had what I considered one of the best doctors in the world, maybe mother's are a tiny bit prejudiced, but he was making a home visit, something doctors don't do anymore. He and Alice arrived a little after twelve and Alice announced she was making dinner for the four of us in celebration. She brought all her ingredients to the kitchen as the doctor set up his few necessary instruments. I couldn't help but have a feeling of pride. He asked me if I was nervous. "Of course not" I said, I've had stitches out before, not on my head of course, but I know it's nothing." Bill, the coward, decided he didn't want to be around so he was going across the street to the park and "smoke a rope", as he called having a cigar. Alice began her work in the kitchen and Rod began his work on my head. He was as gentle as anyone could ever be, asking me periodically if he was hurting me. There were an awful lot of stitches but he completed the job in a short period of time dabbing the approximately fifteen-inch scar with some kind of antiseptic. He kept reminding me that I was his first patient in ten years. I didn't say it to him but I couldn't help thinking what a through and compassionate doctor medicine lost when he choose medical research.

Bill came back just about the time that Alice had dinner ready. We spent a few minutes giving him a bad time about deserting us during the crucial time and then coming back right when the food was ready. I made him look at my beautiful head and of course he said it looked great. Although I wasn't hungry, I did eat as much as I could. The four of us had a good time and a lot of silly laughs. I enjoy that.

They left in the early evening and Bill and I sat comfortably in bed to do our exciting thing, watch TV. The programs were not that great, as usual, but we managed to find an old movie we had seen years ago but forgotten most of it so it was worth watching again. About an hour into the movie, a tingle seemed to go through my left cheek and then it felt numb. The same type feeling in two of my fingers followed this on the left hand. It really frightened me so much that I immediately told Bill about it, while at the same time I tried to move the fingers. In only about a minute I began to feel life coming back into them. What a relief! Bill made me promise to tell him if it happened again. I did not want to call the doctor covering for my doctor at that hour, but maybe in the morning.

I did call the doctor the next morning and was not that comfortable talking with this new doctor whom I had never met. He sounded like he knew very little of my case and was hesitant about making any changes in my medication without seeing me first. I argued that I was not up to going all the way to Boston from the Cape and he was supposed to be overseeing my case. He then consented to call into a local lab to have me get a blood Dilantin level and then he would make a decision based on that. Bill had to take me a couple of towns away to the lab where they drew blood and they would notify the doctor as soon as they had the answer. Meanwhile I was feeling all right except for feeling nauseous all the time. I couldn't help feeling angry with insurance companies who I'm sure made the decision how long patients can spend in the hospital after each type of surgery. As a matter of fact, I felt very angry. When the doctor finally called back he increased my medication quite a bit, having me take 500 mg. then 400 mg. then 300 and stay at the 300. The numbness did not occur again in the next three days. Here I had been thinking that as long as I got through the surgery with no deficits that I was home free. Now I realized that I was still treading on thin ice, that anything could still happen. A little depressing to say the least. Bill took me out for a couple of short rides just to change the scenery and once I even walked over to the park with him while he smoked his rope. On Sunday morning as Bill was getting ready for church I thought to myself, "I think I'd like to go with him." When I announced that I was going to go with him he had the "fit" that I knew he'd have. I went through all kinds of begging telling him how good I felt and that church would be uplifting to me etc. etc. Finally he gave in with the condition that we'd have to sit in the back of the church and I was to tell him if I didn't feel well, even in the slightest way, so we could leave. I consented to everything.

In the church I felt peaceful and happy to be there. I truly felt God's graces and that they would bring about a faster healing. Towards the end of Mass I felt the tingling in my cheek and waited to see if it would start in my fingers. It did and started traveling to the next finger. My thoughts were, "now I'll really notice if it numbs like the last time and then goes away." Instead of the tingling stopping at the second finger it continued to travel to the third, forth, fifth, up into the hand. I was so frightened that it would keep going right up my arm. Before I could even tell Bill tears were falling down my checks. When Bill looked at me he knew full well something was badly wrong. He ushered me out of the church and to the car as I was trying to explain through my tears that my whole hand was numb. Slowly, much more slowly than before, feeling began to come back into my hand, a section at a time I could feel life coming back into the palm, then one finger at a time just as it had left. I was sobbing with gratefulness but somewhat inconsolable. Bill wanted to bring me to the hospital but I just thought calling the doctor would be sufficient since my hand and fingers were again normal.

We called the doctor covering for my doctor again but he was off that Sunday and someone else was covering for him. I felt like asking, "Is this man's greatest hospital?" I was so disgusted; I said, "Never mind." I had made the decision to call my neurologist daughter-in-law. Why hadn't I done this in the first place? I can always get her, at home, in the hospital or on vacation. Bill approved and that's what we did. She immediately sent me for another blood level and found it was low.

She then set up a schedule for my medication for the next three days, starting at 700 mg. the first day and working me down to 400 mg. each day. Then I was to go back to the lab and repeat the process. I felt much better having someone I could talk with. I had many questions at times but hesitated to ask the doctor in case I sounded stupid. Now I felt able to say whatever I was thinking without feeling I'd be put down in any way. I began to feel a little better each day.

My oldest sister, the one whose house we stayed at the night before the surgery, was to celebrate her 50th wedding anniversary in another week. She had been in poor health for the past ten years and we all, including her, felt it was quite a feat that she was able to make it to the 50th. I wanted so much to go as I felt she might not be around for another year. I asked Bill to take me if only for an hour or two if I had no bad episodes for a week. He agreed. I choose a blue dress to wear and I would wear my new hat to cover my bald spot. I remembered the fancy trim that was on the Godiva chocolates that Donald had brought me. I went and got the ribbon and little flower and fruit pieces. I turned one side of the hat up and trimmed it with the chocolate trim. It looked great. The following Saturday we drove off Cape and arrived at the celebration. We had a wonderful time and my sister was so surprised and happy to see me. She never expected I would get there. Pictures were taken of all four girls together. I'm the youngest in a family of four girls. It was a real blessing because four months later my sister died and I will always have that last great memory.

8

BEAUTIFUL FALL

I was awakened from my reveries when I heard Bill's voice saying, "It's getting late, maybe we should head for home."

"Yes, I don't know where the afternoon went, but I think you had a good nap."

"You should talk, I thought you were in another world when I looked at you."

Perhaps I was, I thought to myself. We put the chairs back on the patio, made sure the grill was covered, locked the house and headed for the car for the short trip home.

When we arrived in the house the first thing I did was check the telephone for messages. There was just one. My friend from college days was very ill in the hospital. We immediately called her house and fortunately her husband was at home and was able to give us the details of what happened. It seems she had gone to the hospital for a simple colonoscopy but during the procedure her colon was punctured and poison poured through her body. Instead of being able to come home the same day she was in intensive care with the doctors trying to save her life. We were shocked to hear this. She had been a friend for many years. We had vacationed together with our whole families and spent many New Years Eves together. We had a lot of history. Her husband had said not to visit her, as she was too sick for visitors. I could fully understand that. We sent flowers and prayed, calling every few days to be updated. With each call things seemed a little better. We couldn't help but begin thinking that our friends were beginning to die off and wondered sometimes who would be next. It takes these shocking things to get one to start thinking that way and then the realization that time is passing faster than we would like to think. Here I was complaining about taking so much medicine, but at least I was alive and getting a little stronger each day.

My next visit to Dr. Case was the following Wednesday. I listed all the questions I had and gave them to him one by one. First I wanted to complain about always feeling nauseous. I wondered if eating smaller amounts would help that. He made a call to the blood labs for me to go for another Dilantin level right after meeting with him.

"When can I go swimming?" I asked.

"Whenever you want to."

"Fresh water? Salt water?"

"Both."

I needed prescriptions for pain (mostly to use at night). He wrote them out for me.

"Can I expect to get rid of all symptoms with the medications?"

"Maybe, maybe not, only time will answer that."

"When can I drive?"

"You have to be at least six months seizure free, that's a state law."

"Sometimes I have sensitive feelings, almost like my ear, jaw or right side of my throat are going to ache. Is that related to the tumor?"

"No"

I wasn't totally sure he was right because I never had it before the tumor, but I didn't say it. I went for the blood level and the next day Dr. Case's secretary called saying it was low and I was again to increase the amount of medication. I had told him of my experiences while he was away and that my daughter in law would be my neurologist from then on. He knew that. She had already faxed everything to him.

September was slipping by quickly; we were already into the third week. I had been to one of the shows with Mae and she kidded me about only missing one show through the whole duration of my problems. We gave those tickets to Ben and Bea. My feeling was I'd sit and watch T.V. at home so why not cross the street and sit and watch a show. Good times with friends and family meant a lot to me. There were only two shows a month anyway, six in the course of the summer. We only had one to go. Bill was lucky he had two beautiful women to take to dinner and the show. At least that's what I'd tell him.

That same week, our friend from Danvers was well enough to be discharged from the hospital. We planned a day to go and visit her for just a short while. It was good to see both she and her husband and to know she was going to be all right again. It would take time, but don't all these things. We sat on her deck and talked mostly about how the years have flown. On our way back, Bill and I decided to stop at Kathy's as we practically pass her place going home. She had just returned from work and insisted we stay at least for supper or stay over night and go home the next day. We opted for just supper, as I was uncomfortable enough in my own bed, much less someone else's. Slowly all her family drifted in, her husband and three daughters. We talked about the upcoming wedding. It was a good move to stop there as I think both Bill and I were feeling pretty depressed leaving Danvers.

The weather was beginning to cool on Cape Cod. We went to the lake one of the warmer days but found the water beginning to get pretty cool, especially if you swam out very deep. I was only good for about five minutes of strokes anyway. Much less than my usual half-mile. Maybe I'll work back to it, I'd tell myself. On one raw and cloudy day my energy level was very low, but because of the weather I thought we should get out of the house for a few hours. I suggested we find the Walmarts that is just off Cape in Wareham. We could stroll around and maybe pick up a few things. I was looking for some bird feeders to give as anniversary gifts to our two youngest sons, Scott and Donald. We dressed in slacks, comfortable walking shoes, jackets, and of course my hat. We just got seated in our Chrysler Concorde when Bill started looking in the console between the two front seats for a tape to play some music. He had to move a few other things to get at the tapes and he began looking at titles on the tapes when some of the things on his lap began slipping and started falling. He was grumbling to himself as he started picking things up and trying at the same time to keep more things from falling, when the tape he had chosen slipped behind the console onto the floor of the car. A few choice words joined the grumbling, but I stayed out of it except to tell him the tape was on the floor behind his seat. The next couple of minutes were spent picking things up and straightening the things in the console. He closed the console to begin our ride and when he reached to start the music, discovered there was no tape in the cassette. Staring straight ahead he said out loud, "After all that bullshit don't tell me I didn't even put a tape in!"

He opened the console again to get a tape. I burst out laughing causing him to laugh at himself too. We were off to a great start on this gloomy day.

We decided to take the scenic route. This is a road called King's Highway that was an old carriage road back in the 17th century. Although it's now a fairly busy paved road it still has its old historic charm. The only trouble with traveling this lovely route is that there are few places where one car can pass another. Sometimes this can be pretty frustrating waiting for the really slow car in front of you to take a left or a right to get out of your way. In most places the speed limit is 40 miles an hour, which is comfortable on this beautiful winding road. On our trip we seemed to have several "arssholes" as my driver called them, in front of us going about 20 miles an hour. Toward the end of the road an old lady pulled out of a driveway without even looking and right in front of us. Bill had to jam on the brakes.

"Look at what that old crow did!"

He shouted to no one in particular. Since no damage was done, I asked, "What's the difference between an arsshole and an old crow?"

We both laughed as we continued over the bridge and on to Walmarts.

Life is filled with moments like this in all our lives, but I thank God for the ability to be able to laugh at ourselves. Sometimes I believe laughter is what keeps us going in little annoyances and even more so in the great stresses and sorrows of our lives.

I got the bird feeders. It was time to think about packing for Florida and getting ready for the wedding.

9

THE WEDDING

We had two doctor appointments the following week. I officially got permission to go to Florida for the winter provided I periodically had Dilantin blood levels done and had the results faxed to Dr. Case. Bill had been completely neglected as far as physicals were concerned and I insisted he have at least a few things checked out before we left. The end of the week we enjoyed another show with Mae.

Life went on pretty much as usual the following week. We spent most of our time packing and shopping for the right dress for me to wear to the wedding, after all this was my first grand daughter getting married. I didn't know what I was going to do about my huge bald spot but I knew if I thought long enough that I'd come up with some idea. Donald was faithfully calling every week to ask how I was doing. He is the one in the family that I was always getting after for not checking in on us often enough. I realized how busy he was between work and travel and he had tremendous responsibility, but I would say,"can't you take even five minutes out of your busy life?" Since he heard I had the brain tumor he faithfully called and sometimes I would think that there are a few good things that come out of bad ones if we look for them. Kathy called one week before the wedding and when I picked up the phone and said "hello." I heard her voice saying, "Hi mom, I just called to find out how things are going with the summer from hell?"

I had to laugh as I answered, "That would make a great title for a book."

"Why don't you write it? You know all about it."

"Maybe I will one day."

The bug was in my ear.

One week to get all ready for both the wedding and Florida. My energy level was still pretty low and I had moments when I really felt punk, but we plodded along trying to get everything done. There were lists of all kinds of things that we must not forget if we were to be gone for six months. We couldn't forget important papers, insurance, tax, medical, it seemed to go on and on. Then there were things we'd be apt to walk out without if we didn't check a list such as medicines, special pots and pans that I was so used to using I wanted to use them on both ends. Bill had to change the oil on the car and rotate the tires, check everything about it before we could venture a 1600-mile ride. There is much to do. Clean out the refrigerator, which meant we ate a lot of left overs that week. Bill hated that. He'd say, "throw it out" and I'd keep reminding him of all the hungry people in the world. We went through this little scene twice a year. When we left Massachusetts and when we left Florida. Then there was putting the phone on vacation, canceling the newspaper, forwarding the mail, giving away any plants and it seemed a million other things. There was always the worry that we'd forget to do something important.

On one of our shopping tours I found a little black velvet hat that I thought would match the dress I was going to wear to the wedding. That night I tried on the dress and hat and something wasn't quite right. My dress was quite long so I decided to cut enough off the bottom to make it cocktail length. I fiddled with the piece of material I had taken off the bottom until I figured out a way to make a trim on the hat. Then I was satisfied with my outfit. Shoes, dress, hat and bag all matched.

Bill's plan was that on the day of the wedding we would go to Rod's house. Rod was driving from New York, and he, Alice, Bill and I would go to the church and reception together. We had a key to his house in case we got there before them. We had the car so full we couldn't take anyone with us. The only empty part was the driver's seat and passenger seat in front. We locked the house as we were leaving and gave ourselves plenty of time for the trip. The wedding was at five. We arrived at Rod's about three and about three thirty we decided to change into our wedding clothes in case he and Alice needed to take showers after their long drive, we would at least be out of the way and through using the bathroom. We waited, when at last the phone rang. It was Donald and his wife. They had just flown in from New York and were coming out to Rod's in a rented car. They wanted to be sure they could get in.

"We're here" I told him "but Rod and Alice aren't here yet".

"O.K., we'll see you in about fifteen minutes."

As I hung up the phone, I wondered why Rod and Donald didn't get together on their plans since they were both coming from New York City, but that's kids for you. Donald and Linda arrived as they had said and we all gave each other hugs. We talked awhile, when Donald said, "We better get started changing because we have to take showers."

I looked at my watch and said, "Good God, hurry up, it's 4:15 and Rod and Alice might need the bathroom when they get here."

They headed upstairs and were gone about ten minutes when Rod and Alice arrived. They were really discombobulated. Their car had given them trouble on the way and it delayed them about an hour. Rod was to do a reading at the wedding and he said he hadn't even had a chance to look it over. They needed showers before they got dressed. I was getting more nervous by the minute. You'd think it was my wedding. I told Rod that Donald was in the shower. The next thing I heard was Rod running over the stairs and shouting

"Donald and Linda let out of there."

Bill and I just looked at each other and waited in the kitchen. I kept looking at my watch and getting more nervous. I figured the ride to the church to take about twenty-five minutes and it was already 4:30. About fifteen minutes later 4:45, Donald and Linda came out to the kitchen all dressed up. I was such a wreck that I kept announcing the time. A couple of minutes later Rod and Alice came out. I took a breather to look and think how good-looking they were all dressed up. Rod said, "I can't take my car, I don't trust it."

Donald said, "Come on, we'll take mine. You have to do a reading and I drive faster than Dad. Mom and Dad, You follow in your car."

Bang! The businessman settled everything. Rod hollered back, "Lock the door."

Bill locked the door and we went out to our own car. The other four were gone like the wind. We drove along at a normal rate and even stopped for gas. When we finally got to the church the bride had not yet arrived. This being late for your wedding must be a genetic thing, but somehow it works. We were seated in our seats when the music began and the bride, our granddaughter, looking like a princess came down the aisle on the arm of her proud Dad. What a beautiful wedding it was! Rod did a perfect job of his reading. I never did find out if he ever had a chance to go over it first. Our own daughter, mother of the bride looked so young and lovely, I had to think back to her wedding day and wonder where the years had gone.

We drove ourselves to the reception and on the way I commented to Bill that if we had just planned on going by ourselves in the first place we would have been spared a lot of anxiety. He agreed but couldn't help but notice how the young people just took it all in stride. He wondered if we're just getting old and can't take it anymore. I wondered the same thing.

The wedding was wonderful as weddings usually are, but somehow they are extra special when they're in your own family. It was such fun to see all our nieces, nephews, and families and to watch the young people dance. They mixed the music of today with that of yesterday to give the earlier generation a chance to get out there on the dance floor. Bill had a wonderful time with his sons as I did with my daughters. Some of the boys got Bill into the lounge for a drink and cigar while I was being visited at the table by some of the girls. During this time the band was playing a nice slow number and Donald came along and asked me to dance. I was delighted and had about enough energy to get through a slow dance. For the first time, I realized Donald is a real good dancer and I told him how his father and I used to dance quite often when we were young. He said he loved to dance too, like his Dad. As the number came to an end, he put both arms around me and squeezed me saying, "I love you Mom." I was so overcome with emotion I could hardly get the words, "I love you too" out. I don't think many mothers have a special moment like that.

When the evening was over we drove ourselves back to Rod's house. Donald and Linda dropped Rod and Alice there and were on their way to someone else's house. The four of us hashed over the wedding into the wee hours of the morning. We finally went to bed. We woke to a torrential rainstorm. It was Sunday morning and we usually liked heading for Florida on Sunday in order to get through the New York traffic before the workweek begins. The rain was coming down so hard and so heavy we decided to wait to see if it would let up. More than once we commented on the fact that had it happened yesterday it would have ruined the wedding. The rain and wind kept up through the whole day so our travels would not begin until Monday.

When we woke on Monday morning the sun was shining. We had breakfast, said our good byes and were off for a long trip. Nothing is more beautiful than Fall in New England and I always hate leaving it. Only the thoughts that in another five or six weeks everything could be white with snow make me willing to go. When we were young, white with snow was a welcome sight. We would take the whole family to local ski areas and have some wonderful times. One day a year was set aside for a trip to the mountains. That was a special day that all looked forward to. Now we were trying to enjoy the views of the leaves as they were at their peak of color, traveling through Massachusetts and into Connecticut, upper New York State and into Pennsylvania. We made a brief stop in Connecticut to eat lunch at a rest area, now near the mountains in Pennsylvania we stopped for the night. That was a long enough day for us. Exhausted, we both slept sound and woke ready to start the next day's drive. This routine went on for three more days and nights until we reached the Florida border on the forth day. Each time we do this we think back to the first time. We did the whole trip in two days as if someone was waiting for us and then asked each other why. Now we go leisurely along until we get there.

The first few days we meet with friends from the building and hear the news of the summer. There is always someone who died or had a stroke or some other tragic thing, but there are the happy things too like new grandchildren or someone got married. The news of my brain tumor was perhaps one of the most startling bits of news and I got a million questions and was being asked daily how I felt. Was I upset, or enjoying the attention? I wasn't sure which.

We planned on being in Florida only a week and a half and then flying back to Boston for two days for the reunion. The long awaited reunion was coming up and I would have another reason to wear what I called, "my wedding dress."

10

THE REUNION

I was taking four capsules each day consisting of 100 mg. each. The doctor had only ordered me to take the 400 mg. each day and it did not matter whether I took them with food or not. Most mornings I would wake feeling nauseous. I felt like a pregnant woman again waking with that awful feeling like I was going to throw up, but I never threw up. I started playing with my medication, wondering if I should take it on an empty stomach or wait until I'd eaten something before taking the first capsule. After awhile I discovered that I could somewhat control the seizures by taking a capsule as soon as I felt the risings coming on. My energy level was extremely low and I would sleep 12 and 14 hours a night. I think I would have stayed in bed all day if Bill didn't wake me and tell me to come for breakfast. Ordinarily I've been one who woke early and was raring to go. What a difference. The doctor had said it would be at least a year before I was feeling more like myself and I had to keep reminding myself of that. I was sure in time that would all change.

Our condo in Florida is right on the ocean and I've always been a beach lover. Bill and I differ on that too. He's a fresh water fan, but he does enjoy walking on the beach. I hadn't gone in the ocean the whole first week because the waves were so strong and my balance still wasn't what it used to be. One beautiful day the ocean looked so inviting. The waves were big puffs of water not breaking until they were close to shore. I couldn't resist the blue water calling me to get into it. Bill and I were on the boardwalk that goes over the dunes. A bench is built on both sides where people from the condo can sit and look at the sea. We watch all the space shots from that area, as we're just a short distance from the Kennedy Space Center. A night shot is something to behold. As the rocket ascends, night is turned into day as the light streams into the sky. We can see the boosters as they separate from the shuttle. But I digress. We were sitting there. I was in a bathing suit and I said to Bill, "I think I'll go in the water." "You be careful, those waves are stronger than you think." I shuffled through the sand to the water's edge. It felt so good on my feet. I gradually started walking in with the intention of getting past the area where the waves were breaking and floating on the swells. When I reached a depth of about hip deep a wave broke. Much to my surprise it knocked me down. Before I could get myself up another wave hit me. I was frightened and struggled to pull myself up. Bill had seen it. He came running down but I was just about up when he reached the water and I ran toward him. "You're not quite up to that yet," he said. "I guess not," I answered. I felt like crying knowing that to get past those waves only a few months before would have been no problem for me. We stood at the water's edge for a while when a big burley man from our condo came from nowhere out of the water. He loved the ocean like I do and said, "Have you been in Helen? The water is beautiful." We both answered together telling him how I tried but couldn't get past the breakers. "Come on, lean on my arm. I'll get you in there." Bill didn't think I should, but I still wanted to float over the waves so I accepted the invitation. Once I was by the rough area I just lay in the water looking up at the clouds in the sky. The clouds in the Florida sky make all different formations with streaks of red and blue running through them. I spent ten or fifteen minutes in ecstasy, floating and looking, better than any tranquilizer could ever be. When I made my way out of the water, I noticed that Bill had stayed right on the edge ready to run in and grab me even in all his clothes if I had any difficulties. For the first time in my adult life I felt like I must be physically dependent, but then I went back to reminding myself that it would be at least a year.

We had our tickets to fly back to Boston for the reunion and return tickets to come back the next day. We had our reservations at the Inn where the celebration was to take place and now it was time to start thinking of packing. It could be cool or even cold in New England this time of year so we had to prepare. Although we'd only be there for an overnight we still needed clothes for the dinner banquet and leisure clothes for the next morning. There was to be a Mass at five o'clock at the church in the parish where we all went to school and then we would all go to the Inn in Lexington about fifteen miles away where the dinner was planned. I figured that everyone would arrive at the Mass in the clothes they would wear all evening, so I made plans to go to another sister's house just long enough to change from our travel clothes to our dress clothes. She lives quite close to the church so that should work out fine. Early Saturday morning we set out for the Orlando Airport to take an 11:30 flight. I wore slacks and a lightweight shirt and carried a jacket for later in the journey. Of course I had to pack a dressy jacket for the evening, and Bill had to pack a suit, shoes, tie, the works, so we weren't exactly traveling light. I had decided that wearing my good jewelry was the safest way to bring it. I had on my 22 carrot gold earrings that Bill had given me as a gift. I seldom wore them for fear of loosing them. I seem to have a habit of loosing one earring. That was why I got my ears pierced some twenty years ago, but it didn't solve the problem. Somehow I still manage to knock out the stud that holds them on and periodically I still lose an earring. I put my jewelry on with great care and checked with my fingers every so often to make sure it was all still in tact.

We arrive at the airport and parked the car in the garage. We did the usual standing in line, Bill shoving our bag in front of us as we progressed. After a fashion we reached the counter to check our bags, answer whether we were carrying any packages for strangers and all the rest of the new safety things that have been put into place since so many crazys have been running around the country. Then came the part where we had to show picture identification. Bill opened his wallet to show his license. That was fine. I opened my checkbook holder where I put all my cards including my license. I flipped it in front of the clerk. He looked and said; "I can't read this." I thought to myself, "*what is wrong with this moron?*"

"Why not?" I asked. "I can't." he answered exasperatingly. I pulled the folder back and looked. There was my driver's license from the Middle East where we lived the last two years of Bill's work life. It was all in Arabic. I carried it under my Florida license just because I thought it was unique and of course I can't drive now so I wasn't sure where I had put my Florida license. I started to get all flustered and hunting through my cards for the license I could feel myself sweating with nerves. People in the line behind were getting impatient too. Bill was asking me what I did with my license and that didn't help either because I didn't know. Finally I found a student I.D. from the local college, left from some courses we had taken there. The clerk said, "There's no picture on it." In desperation I asked, "Can't you use the picture from this," pointing to the Arabic license "and the information from this" pointing to the student I.D. In disgust, he finally consented; clearly letting me know it was not regulation. We got our tickets and our bag checked.

We headed for the gate where the plane going to Boston would be landing. I went in and used the ladies room and came back to one of the seats in the waiting area. Bill asked me what had happened to my license and I started going through my checkbook again. Then I dug into my pocket book for my wallet, which I never used for anything but bills. There right in front was my driver's license. As I looked at it I remembered putting it there sometime in the summer when I was going out to a store and didn't want to bring a pocket book. I just put the license in the wallet just in case I needed it. Well, thank heaven at least I had it. We talked about having a rather bad start but hoped it was not a premonition of the weekend to come. Just about the time people were beginning to be called to board the plane, I reached to check my earrings. One was missing. I panicked. It must be somewhere right around here as I began looking on my clothes and the seat and the floor. Bill was beside himself with me. He helped me look and at the same time kept telling me our row would be called real soon. "I can't go without my earring," I said. "We won't get there if you don't," he said as we continued to look. Just as our seating row was called, Bill said, "here it is." He picked it up from the floor and handed it to me. I was so grateful, I nervously gathered my belongings and we filed in line to get on the plane.

Bill put the carry on bag in the upper compartment and we settled into our seats, glad to finally be on our way. I sat at the window seat and watched as the plane climbed into the sky making our world below look like a miniature board game. This would be about a three-hour straight through flight. About noontime we all were given our "yummy" airplane lunch. We ate enough to hold us over until the banquet that evening. An hour into the flight I was ready to fall asleep. As my eyes were drooping something seemed to run down my blouse. I thought it was some kind of bug, but it happened so fast I didn't really get a look at it. I searched around my lap, but found nothing. I tried looking down on the floor but the seats are so close together, as anyone who has ever been in coach in a plane will agree, but I thought I saw something like a pearl. I unfastened my seat belt to be able to lean way over and reach the item. Bill said, "What the heck are you doing?" In my stretched over position, I said, "I'm Getting something." It took all the stretch of my body and fingers to reach it, but I finally was able to grab the object and pull myself up to a normal seating position. Then I was able to look more closely at what I had in my hand. As I looked, my tongue ran over my teeth and immediately I knew. It was the crown that was put right in the front of my mouth when I was only eighteen years old. This was the last straw. With tears in my eyes I pointed out what had happened. Bill started to try to calm me by saying we'd find a dentist as soon as we landed in Boston. "Oh sure, Saturday afternoon and we're going to find a dentist in his office, besides we don't have enough time, maybe I can stick it back in. It's bad enough to go to my 50th reunion with a half bald head but now I have a tooth missing from the front of my mouth." "Don't be so upset," Bill said, "we'll find some solution." By this time I couldn't sleep or read or anything else. I could only feel bad for myself. I carefully put the crown in a safe place in my pocketbook. I sat there praying for a solution and sulking like a spoiled kid, but I thought I deserved the right to sulk.

When the plane began to descend and I could see Boston Harbor, I thought I had a brilliant idea. "I've got it," I said to Bill, "I've got the solution. We can stop in a drug store and buy some of that stuff people use to glue in their false teeth. That should work." I felt pleased as punch with myself for thinking it up. "I think you've got something there he said, that's what we'll do." I could feel myself beginning to relax again, but what else could happen this day.

The plane landed safely and at least we weren't in a plane crash. These kinds of thoughts made my problems seem minuscule, and that's how I needed to think. After getting our baggage from the carousel we headed to the car rental area where we had reserved a car. There was a line of people and Bill got at the end of the line, which kept growing, around him. One girl was taking care of the customers while another fellow talked on the phone. Eventually it was Bill's turn and when he reached the counter, the girl said, "Go over there to him." So Bill gentlemanly stepped to the fellow. He kept talking and people who were behind Bill were being taken care of. I was sitting on a bench nearby and could see Bill getting angry and I must say, I felt the same way. Finally the guy hung up the phone. He couldn't find our reservation and said we could have whatever car they might happen to have. Bill is getting furious, "I had a reserved car and that's what I want," his voice raising. "O.K., O.K." handing him a set of keys he said, "There's one parked out by that pole. Bill grabbed the keys after signing all the papers and stomped away with me following. The car was filthy dirty. Bill said, "look at this filthy car." Because Time was passing he opened the door. The inside was worse than the outside. It had not been cleaned from the last people. There were paper cups on the floor, all kinds of junk around. Bill slammed the door and headed back into the building. He shouted at the clerk that the car was filthy. "That's the car you wanted," the clerk said with a sarcastic grin. "Where's the manager?" Bill shouted. By this time everyone was looking at him. The girl Pointed to a nearby door and Bill went storming in. The next thing I knew the car was cleaned both inside and out in record time and we were at last headed for Cambridge.

I wanted to stop someplace to buy the glue, or whatever; to fix my tooth but Bill thought it was so late that we should wait until after the Mass. We headed straight for my sister's house to change clothes, and as I washed my face and renewed my make up I would smile into the mirror and wonder how I would get through even the Mass without someone seeing me look like a Halloween pumpkin. Bill said, "You don't talk during Mass." "But what am I supposed to do when Mass is over and people start recognizing each other and everyone is gabbing." "We'll have to save our gabbing for when we get to the Inn." As soon as we were all dressed up, we said good-bye and headed for the church. As we turned into the parking lot, I noticed a WHITE HEN PANTRY across the street. "There's a store, I'll run over and see if I can get something." "They won't have what you're looking for, you need a drug store." "You never know, I'll give it a try." Bill reluctantly crossed the street with me and we went into the store. We looked around and could find nothing. "I knew they wouldn't have it, let's go." "Wait, I'll ask that clerk." I explained my dilemma to the girl and she said she thought they had something that would do the trick. She looked, I prayed. "Try this", she said as she handed me a small box with a small tube inside. I thanked her and paid for it, only $2.50. I would have spent ten times that for an answer to my problem. We crossed back across the street and I headed for the car. "Where are you going now?" "Back to the car so I can look in the mirror and try to put this tooth in." I got into the car and opened the package, putting a little of the cement on the top of my crown; I pushed it tight into my gum. It seemed to be staying in place. With a sigh of relief I said, "I think it's going to work." We went into the church and looked at all these old people that we were young with fifty years ago. One of our classmates who had been a priest for years said the Mass. He talked about our old high school days and I'm sure I wasn't the only one that was brought back in time. For the next 24 hours we would all be young again.

At the Lexington Inn we checked into our rooms, left our luggage and went immediately to the dining hall where our dinner would take place. We were given name tags with our old high school pictures on them. A very good idea. All evening I found myself and noticed others too peeking at the name tags as we conversed with each other. I was the only one wearing a hat and I know the reason why was spread rapidly through the room. I immediately changed the order I had made for dinner. I had specified beef when I sent back my reservations, but decided to change it to chicken in the hopes that my tooth could handle the chicken. With beef I might just say good-bye to it again. I'd had enough trouble for one day or at least I thought so. Then I said to Bill, "Where is my camera?" "I don't know, don't you have it?" I went back to the room to see if I left it with my luggage, but it wasn't there. I sat on the edge of the bed trying to retrace my steps as to when I last remembered having had it. I recalled carrying it through the X Ray area at the airport and hanging it on the back of the door in the airport bathroom. I must have come out without taking it off the door. I began to get upset because it was practically new. Bill had given it to me in the summer as an early birthday gift because I broke my other camera. I hated to have to tell him. Back in the function room I broke the news of the camera to him. I knew by the look on his face he was a bit disturbed with me but it had been such a hectic day he said, "There's nothing we can do about it now. On our way back we'll check and see if it got turned in. Don't let it spoil your reunion." We both knew there wasn't much chance it would be turned in, but I was determined to enjoy all my old friends and forget about all the hassles of getting there.

The evening turned out to be wonderful. I spent time with some of my best friends in high school but had lost touch with through the years. I knew we would now renew old acquaintance for whatever time we had left. My tooth behaved itself. There was a tribute to all those that had died and it was a shock to most of us at the number who had passed on. It was a reality of the brevity of life. Many stayed up half the night but I wasn't up to that. Plans were made for all of those who were staying over to meet for breakfast the next morning, and the next morning we just did it all over again.

In the afternoon we headed again for the airport. We flew out of Boston at 2:30 and arrived back in Florida around 5:30. The first thing I did was to check the lost and found about my camera, but as expected it was not there. I left my name and address so it could be returned if it was turned in but of course I had little hope of that happening. We got our own car from the garage and drove home talking all the way of what a good time we had. All the negative things faded into the distance in favor of the positives. It was dark when we arrived home. We both agreed that the hectic couple of days were well worth the pleasure of being with old friends. Remembering the days when we were all carefree; before responsibilities to families, before the pain of the death of loved ones, before the million struggles of life, sickness, job losses, the fears of tomorrow. In a sense, we were young again for a little while.

11

SUMMER'S OVER

November is here already. Officially summer is over and winter is close in the northeast, but here in Florida we still have warm weather and this often confuses me about the seasons.

My first move on our return trip was to make a dentist appointment. My thinking was that one appointment would be all I'll need to get my crown cemented back in, but nothing seems to be that simple. After I entertained everyone in the office by telling them of the dilemma I was in by having the crown break off at such an inopportune time and their laughter subsided, I got examined. My dentist informed me that the part of the tooth that the crown was attached to had partially broken off. This left me with two choices. 1. Go to a Periodotist and have my gum cut so that my dentist has more of an area to work with, or 2. Have the root removed and have a false tooth bridged in its place. My first thought was, "I don't want a false tooth." I told my dentist my feelings and so she made an appointment for me with a peridontist.

At home Bill and I discussed this new mess I was in. He suggested I might look like Peter Rabbit with part of my gum higher than the rest. I thought about it for a few days. During this time, mild seizures were beginning to be more frequent. That meant I needed another blood Dilantin level. So there are two appointments. All that so-called retirement fun seems to be being spent with doctors and dentists, and I don't mean socially. I got the blood level test and once again the pills I had managed to decrease to 300 mg. a day went back to 400 mg. a day. One-step forward, two backwards. Discouraging! My emotions are on one long roller coaster ride, up, down, up, down, with very little time spent in between. All this time I was thinking about looking like Peter Rabbit, so I decided to cancel my appointment with the peridontist and go the other route.

Meanwhile time is passing and our youngest son Donald is planning Thanksgiving at his apartment in Manhatten. Am I going to have my tooth fixed in time? So much seems to be happening and I'm always so tired. My dentist explained that the root could be extracted the next week but I'd have to wait three or four more weeks for the gum to heal before the new tooth could be put in. Meanwhile she would take impressions and have the new tooth ready by the time my gum was healed. She would put some kind of temporary tooth in immediately and she assured me it would look good and I could eat with it. The darn tooth seemed to be as much trouble as the brain tumor, but not quite as worrisome.

Donald sent airline tickets to us to go to New York so with or without energy, I planned on going.

The night before Thanksgiving we packed our bags. After a short nights sleep we rose early to have breakfast, showers and get out by 6:15. We drove to Orlando Airport for the second time in three weeks. We left our car at a nearby parking lot because on Thanksgiving weekend all parking garages are pretty much filled up. Shuttles are provided to take people to the airport from parking lots that are a few miles away so we felt relieved to even get a parking spot on such a busy weekend. This time I made sure I had the right license in my pocket book and tried not to repeat all the faux pas I made on the last trip. We dressed in slakes and carried a winter jacket to put on at the other end. The few weeks since our last trip really made a difference in the weather up north. Winter had reared its ugly head and the icy winds were blowing. About two and half-hours into the trip the pilot said, "The winds were in our favor." We gathered all our belongings, including a half-bushel of oranges I had convinced Bill we should bring and disembarked. Off we went to the baggage area. At the baggage area we saw a chauffeur with a sign with our name on it. "Good God," I said, "I haven't seen that since we were in the Middle East. Donald had said he would send a driver to pick us up because he would be busy getting the turkey ready. Bill and I did a lot of joking between us after that conversation and I told him I was born too soon. I guess I envied the gals of this generation getting help with the cooking, cleaning and everything else. We approached the driver and identified ourselves. He took most of the bags and we followed him to a town car where he put everything in the trunk, remarking how good the oranges looked. The bag was beginning to break from lugging it around. We just about made it before having oranges all over the street.

The ride to Donald's apartment was only about a half-hour away. Our driver had to weave in and out of streets because so many were shut off because of the big Thanksgiving Day parade. There was our son waiting in front of his building for us to arrive. He paid the driver as I handed him a couple of the oranges. Donald looked wondering what that was all about but the driver gave me a big smile. As we went into the building I explained to Donald how the driver thought those oranges looked so good as he put them into the trunk. Donald laughed and I detected a look on his face that kind of said, "Only you!" We took the elevator to the thirtieth floor. What a view we had from his apartment, across the street was the Lincoln Center and out the side was the ABC building. We were the last ones of the expected guests to arrive for the Thanksgiving celebration so the first half-hour was spent greeting and kissing all the others who could be there. Donald called me into the kitchen to see the turkey. He had bought a special fresh one and beside it I saw a huge bowl of stuffing. Everything was still raw and I said, "You haven't even got it in the oven yet!" "We're not going to eat until about five o'clock," he said, "but don't worry we're going to have all kinds of appetizers. No one will starve." "That stuffing looks great. It's not like mine." "No, it's a recipe I got out of the <u>Golden Palate</u>." I was familiar with the new, yuppie cookbook but had no intention of getting one myself. My days for all that fussing are over.

The afternoon was spent gabbing and eating. Linda was a great hostess while Donald labored in the kitchen not wanting anyone to bother him. I knew my kids could cook but this was unbelievable. The young girls, our grand children, set the table with the new china, candles, fine crystal, the works. I guessed that Donald and Linda were perhaps setting out their wedding gifts for the first time. At least for this many people. No gourmet restaurant could have put out a finer meal; with fine wines and just about everything anyone could want. The stuffing was so delicious I had to ask for the recipe. He gave me the cookbook opened to the stuffing. As I scanned the many ingredients, I noticed it called for filbert nuts and I asked Donald what kind of nuts they were. He went into the kitchen and came back with a full bag of the nuts and handed them to me. "If you're going to make the dressing mom, take those nuts home with you." "O.K. I'll try it for Christmas." Maybe I'm not totally finished with some fancy cooking after all.

It was a long day and by the time Kathy and her family left to spend the night at Rod's apartment, I was well ready to turn in.

The plan was that the next day Donald and Linda would bring all of us up to Larchmont where they had just purchased a house. They had not yet moved in as they were doing extensive renovations and wanted it all done before they moved in. We were then to come back and change to go out to dinner and then on to a Broadway show. That was almost too much excitement for me in one day but at the same time I didn't want to miss any of it. We got a good night sleep and ate breakfast. Donald went "out for a run" and Linda went "to exercise" and I was getting tired just watching. Bill and I took it easy for a couple of hours. When they returned the phone started ringing with plans about who would drive and when and where we would all get together. In New York there is no place to park a car and wait for people so it all had to be carefully planned. It was, and we all got together and headed for Larchmont. All of us owwed and ahhed going through the house as Linda and Donald explained what was being done. One room on the first floor was to be the guestroom with a private bath and Donald said,

"Next year when you come for Thanksgiving this will be your room."
We kidded him saying, "We just might move in for good." Then it was
off to a little local restaurant for lunch. By the time we went back to
the apartment to change our clothes then headed to a restaurant in
Manhattan for dinner I was getting exhausted. We devoured a meal fit
for a king and looked like a mob scene in the restaurant. Then it was
head for the theater. Eleven tickets to <u>SHOWBOAT</u> and we all had
great seats. I had never seen it before but I saw the movie years ago and
of course I knew all the songs. I was so tired I had to fight to stay awake
and I think I did it softly singing along with the singers. After the show
as we told Donald how much we enjoyed it he said, "I heard you singing all the songs." "Oh heavens", I thought, "I hope no one else heard
me." It was a wonderful but long day and the bed felt good as I lay my
head on it to get a sound night's sleep.

The next morning we just had a nice slow start. Breakfast with
Linda and Donald and then we packed our things to head back.
Donald drove us to the airport where we said our good byes and before
we knew it we were on the plane heading back to Florida. It all felt like
waking from a dream. It took me the rest of November to get over all
the excitement I had. I had no complaints. My tooth had stayed in and
I would soon be getting my permanent one. My seizure feelings were
kept in check with my medicine. Now all we had to think of was to
start getting ready for Christmas.

A few days after our return, a friend in the condo where we live
offered a group of us some very good prices on a four night, five-day
cruise. This offer usually came up each year in January and each year
we would say to each other that we must go sometime but never did. I
guess all that had taken place in the summer made us realize that next
year may never come so we decided to go. I'd have two weeks to rest up
and get ready for it, besides everyone that had been on cruises before
said you rest on a cruise if you want to. We had never taken a cruise
before so here was another first for me. I would have my tooth put in
before it was time to leave so all should be fine.

Every year when it's time to buy Christmas gifts Bill wants to pick out things from the L.L.Bean catalogue, but I enjoy going through the stores and picking out things I think each one will like. We always argue about the pros and cons of being able to just make a call and have it delivered straight to the person verses picking it out, wrapping and mailing it. He argues the simplicity of doing it his way and I argue that I want to see what I'm sending and I don't mind wrapping and mailing it. Usually we wind up doing some of both. This year, much to Bill's dismay, I didn't give him any argument. I was just too tired to go out in the crowds and shop. Bill was delighted. I even told him to pick the gifts. I must admit we got our shopping done pretty fast, but I did miss hitting some of those stores for before Christmas sales.

My sister Marion was again in the hospital. She had been so sickly for the past ten years that it was not unusual to hear that she was back in the hospital. Being so far away I would make my visits by telephone. She would always say, "Oh Honey, (I was called Honey when I was little and everyone dropped it as I grew except Marion) it's so good to hear your voice." I loved it and we would enjoy a telephone visit. This particular time we talked about her 50th party. It had made her so happy it was almost all she could think of. When she got home from the hospital she was going to sort pictures and send me and my other sisters pictures of us all together. Then on a serious note she said, "Honey, sometimes I feel like this is the beginning of the end." I found myself not disagreeing with her as I often felt that way too. I just said, "Do your best to hang in a little longer and leave the rest to God." "That's exactly how I feel," she said. I hung up the phone feeling a little melancholy.

12

LIVING, HOPING,
DREAMING

By the first week in December I was beginning to feel pretty good as long as I was faithful to my medicine. I did have one episode when part of my left hand became numb but it came back so I didn't bother to say anything to anyone. I knew I was to have another blood level done and it turned out to be in the right range. I went to my dentist and had my permanent tooth put in. I didn't feel as comfortable with it as I had with my crown, but I knew my decision had been made and I had to stick with it. I kind of took it easy, writing Christmas cards and thinking about what I'd bring on the cruise for clothes. I called my sister weekly.

She had been moved to a rehab hospital. That felt a little encouraging. After hanging up the phone I went out to the living room to watch TV. Bill came in from the kitchen with some Clark bars and asked me if I wanted one. I said I would have one. MMM the chocolate tasted good. I bit it to get at the peanut buttery center and snap! My new tooth broke off. I could have cried. At the same time I was ready to kill myself for being so stupid as to bite right on the new tooth. Next morning it's back to the dentist. I felt like a fool when asked what happened, but I was totally honest.

"What kind of candy was it?" she asked.

When I told her she said at least it was a tasty one, she liked them too. This put me at ease and she went to work fixing the tooth only this time she used something that she burnt on. I thought I was being soldered. She said, "It won't come out now."

We left for the cruise on the 8th of December. My seizures had been kept to the minimum so I was looking forward to a good time. Another couple from our condo was joining us. We live in Cocoa Beach so the port is only a few miles away in Cape Canaveral. Before the ship even started to sail we were eating. To me the ship was huge although many people who have done a lot of cruising called it small. I figured it would take me the whole time just finding my way around. Fortunately for us our staterooms were on the Restaurant deck. It had a bathroom with shower and a porthole that I loved climbing up to look out at the wake the ship made in the water. We were assigned tables in the dining room and we choose the early seating. I'm sure many of the younger people were up half the night but I wasn't quite up to that. There was entertainment every night after dinner. Very good entertainment I might add.

By morning the ship had pulled into Nassau. We were offered several different ways to spend our day. I didn't think I should go scuba diving, at least not this year. The couple we were with had been to Nassau before so we decided to just let them be our guide. We went to Paradise Island and sat around the beach and pool, but then decided we can do that right at home in Florida, so we opted for a little shopping and they wanted to go into one of the gambling halls. Bill and I are not much for gambling but we were on vacation so we consented to give the gambling hall ten dollars each and then quit. That took about five minutes. It was a fun day and we headed back to do what? Why eat of course! Tonight was the captain's dinner so everyone got all dressed up and we lined up to meet the captain before dinner. The red carpet was rolled out in every sense of the word. A photographer was there and took a picture of each couple, individual or group as they entered the dining room. The pictures would later be displayed somewhere on the ship for purchase, but no one was obliged to buy them so if you looked a mess you could just leave and forget it. They must file an awful lot of pictures in the trash. We literally stuffed ourselves again with another gourmet meal as the waiters entertained us during dessert and coffee. Too much of this and we would never go back to waiting on ourselves. Our waiter practically begged us to attend the midnight buffet. We tried to tell him we could not eat another bite, but he insisted we should go even if we don't eat because everything is set up so beautifully. We had to say we would try to stay up for it, even though we knew it wouldn't happen. We headed for the Lounge deck where the entertainment was to take place. It lasted from eight to nine thirty; the late dinner crowd would see the same show from ten to eleven thirty. They'll be the ones that will go to the buffet. I must say that those cruise ships hire some really good entertainers. We had singing, dancing, comedians, and even a very good ventriloquist during our stay on board. By the time the show was over we were ready to turn in for the night and slept right through the ship's sailing around the Bahamas to bring us near another port by morning. After breakfast if we wanted to go ashore we were to line up on a particular deck where we boarded a smaller boat called a tender which would bring us to shore. This island was smaller and had no ports large enough to accommodate a large ship, hence the tender boats. We were told that boats would be running every half-hour with the last one leaving at five thirty, so passengers were advised not to miss that one or they would have to swim back to the good old USA. Our group left about ten thirty and planned on returning about three. This island had a diminutive beauty about it, with its little shops and houses painted in various colors along a jagged coastline. We sauntered along going in and out of shops being stopped every twenty steps or so with natives wanting to braid our hair. None of us had the courage to go back to the ship with a million little braids in our hair, but we bought little trinkets and such to take home. Someone had the bright idea to take a bus to another beach that is supposed to be quite beautiful. We asked one of the conductors at the bus station which bus to take and he said to take bus 6. We did. We certainly got a tour of the island because there were no other tourists on that bus but the four of us. It ran through every back road there must have been on that island, bouncing all the way. We must have been on it forty-five minutes when we finally came to the end of the line. We asked how we would get to the special beach and were told we'd have to take a taxi over the bridge to get there. We all decided we should have taken the taxi in the first place, but I bet we saw parts of the island no tourist ever sees. We saw the poverty that is behind the tourist area.

Finally, at the beach we sat and watched as money flowed like water among the visitors and we had to think of our bus ride. Most of the employment on these little islands is catering to tourists. Without tourist trade I don't know how they would live. The hotels are the finest and beautiful condominiums line much of the shore. It is surely a have, have not existence.

We caught our three o'clock tender back to the ship giving us plenty of time to change before dinner. My advice to anyone taking a cruise is to lose five or ten pounds before going. I wished I had realized how wonderful all the food would be. Everyone telling you is not the same as experiencing it. We spent the next day enjoying the amenities right on the ship, lounging around on the pool deck and finding our way to areas we didn't have time to look for before. The next day we would be docking and heading back to reality but with great memories and a few pictures to help those memories.

When we pulled into our garage and entered the building I could not have dreamed of what would await me. As soon as we dropped our entire luggage Bill said, "Check the phone for messages while I open the curtains".

I pushed the message button and heard my sister Ginny's voice saying that she'd call me back. Second message, the same voice saying she had something important to tell me. I began to feel nervous. All these messages were last night and this morning. Third message was, "I have to tell you that Marion died last night."

Although I knew she had been sick I still found it hard to believe she had actually died. Bill came in just as I was listening to the last message.

"We should go up," he said.

"Absolutely, I'll call Ginny and find out the details." Marion had taken a bad turn and was brought back into the hospital. She was coming along pretty well when her heart just gave out. The wake and funeral were to be in the next couple of days. Bill got on the phone and got us reservations for the next day. Almost in a daze I unpacked and re-packed with clothes suitable for up north and for a funeral. As I went to bed that night I could not but remember the words of Kahlil Gibran when he wrote of Joy and Sorrow.

> *"Some of you say, Joy is greater than*
> *Sorrow and others say nay, sorrow is the greater.*
> *But I say unto you, they are inseparable.*
> *Together they come, and when one sits alone*
> *With you at your board, remember that the other*
> *Is asleep upon your bed."*

How true.

I had much to do. We would be catching our plane in early afternoon. First I called Kathy. I could always depend on her to come through in all circumstances. When I told her of her Aunt's death and of the arrangements she said, "I won't be able to go. I have to go to a two day School thing with Em, I promised her and she's been looking forward to it. I'm sorry Mom, I'll send flowers."

Flowers! I hadn't even thought of them.

"Well would you send flowers from the family and let your sister and brothers know. I'll call Rod so we can use their house for a couple of nights if you call the others." "I'll take care of that Mom and I am sorry."

"You can only do so much."

I hung up the phone and called Rod. Alice told me that he was up at Cornell and wouldn't be back for five days, but to go ahead and use the house, the only one that might come in would be a real estate agent. They had moved to New York shortly after my brain surgery and the house was up for sale, but we still had a key. Alice had left most of their furniture in it and we'd only be there for two nights. That meant that Rod wouldn't get to the funeral either. My two most faithful ones for family things wouldn't be there. I felt bad but I could understand. I had taken a good chunk out of their work lives when I had my surgery. Again I thought to myself, "You can only do so much."

We arrived in Boston about three in the afternoon, rented a car and headed directly for Quincy, hoping to get to the funeral parlor before afternoon hours were over. We dressed appropriately at home knowing there would be no time to change clothes. The afternoon hours were from two to four and we did get a little confused finding the right street, so by the time we arrived everyone was leaving. My brother in law, nieces and nephew all insisted we make a quick visit and go back to the house with them so we could return for the evening hours. We said we would do that. I looked at my sister lying in her coffin looking so peaceful I felt as if she were there with me in spirit making me strong. How I loved her.

We went back to her house and it seemed so strange not to have her there trying to make everyone comfortable, but it was also an opportunity to talk with the family and hear all the details of what had happened. They were all so pleased that we had come up from Florida, but how could we not? Nita, my niece said we had just missed Mary at the wake. She had come in the afternoon and left shortly before we arrived. I was so happy to hear that, knowing that Kathy and Rod and probably Donald would not be able to make it. My thoughts were, "*dear Mary, at least she came through.*" I hoped that Scott might show up that night.

We all went back to the funeral parlor for the night calling hours and reality was beginning to set in. My sister was really gone and I would not see her or hear her gentle voice again in this life. It was difficult to internalize. Death was no stranger to me. Only our faith carried us through these traumatic times. I visited and talked to my other two sisters and many cousins and as I spent time alone contemplating the whole ritual we were all attending I had to think of the changes time has made in people's lives. We no longer live in a village being supported by relatives when things go wrong or celebrating with them when things are wonderful. Today the world is at our fingertips for jobs, vacations and living. While we gain much, we also pay the price of families and relatives losing touch with each other. If we're lucky we may gather together at a wedding or funeral. Life is a trade off, we gain, and we lose. None of my large family was there tonight to support me. Well at least Mary had come. Maybe tomorrow at the funeral! I got up and walked toward the casket stopping several feet from it, just looking. My niece Nita came and stood beside me.

"I'll miss her," I said.

"We'll all miss her," she answered.

In my mind I kept thinking I'd never hear her tell me, "Oh Honey, it's so nice to hear your voice," again.

We drove back to Rod's house to get a night's sleep. What a difference a day makes. It was a somber night.

We rose early the next morning to shower and dress for the funeral. This time we had no trouble finding the funeral home. We just had time for a final prayer when names began to be called for the funeral procession to the church. I looked around hoping to see one of my children, but none were there. When our name was called and we began to leave to get in our car, I saw Scott rushing through the parking lot. My heart leaped with joy to know that he had made the trip from Rhode Island. We got together with him at the cemetery though we did see each other at the church. His first words were, "Where's Rod? Where's Kathy?"

We explained why each were not there and he told us that Donald was also traveling for work and couldn't make it either. We hugged him and told him how much it meant to us that he was there and that Mary had been to the wake.

Everyone was invited back to my sister's house from the cemetery. Funny how we Christians always gather for a social time after a loved one is buried. I guess the custom developed from the origins of our belief that we celebrate our loved one entering eternal life, the reason for which we are born. It doesn't deter from our grief or mourning but somehow the strength we gain from sharing our sorrow with other loved ones, of just being together, seems to help. Scott was able to visit with cousins, aunts and uncles he hadn't seen for a long time and we were proud and happy to have him there with us. Strange how much little things mean to us, as we get older. Many had been at the fiftieth Anniversary party only three months before. Sometimes I think my sister fought the good fight long enough to reach that milestone.

In the middle of the afternoon everyone began to say their good-byes until each in turn was left with their own thoughts and realization of their own mortality. We kissed Scott and told him to be careful driving home, as we knew he was very tired. He had been "on call" all night at the hospital before driving to Massachusetts to the funeral. We headed north, back to Rod's house. The next morning we would be flying back to Florida. We were pretty tired too.

We arrived at Orlando airport about three in the afternoon and after getting our car and driving home it was close to five o'clock before we arrived home. It felt so good to be back in our own condo again. It would take awhile before we'd be over this entire running around. But within the week our life began to work its way back to normal. Christmas was only a week away and Bill didn't want to bother getting any decorations out. "Nobody will be here," he said. My energy level felt like agreeing with him, but years ago I used to look at older people who just didn't bother and I promised myself I wouldn't get like that. "We'll just put up the nativity set and the ceramic Christmas tree," I said. So we dragged the boxes from way back in the closet and at least made the place look a little like Christmas.

"Where do you want to go for Christmas dinner," Bill said. I thought about it for awhile and then said, "You know, I think I'd like to cook that turkey I have in the freezer and we can just have a quiet Christmas here at home. The kid's will all be calling up and we'll be here to get the calls. That's what I'd like this year."

"Whatever you want. I just thought you might want to get waited on instead of cooking."

"You can help me make Donald's fancy stuffing."

I pulled the turkey from the freezer to give it a few days to thaw in the refrigerator.

On the day before Christmas we planned to go to the Vigil Mass at ten at night and we would make the stuffing so it would be ready to put into the bird first thing in the morning. I had all the many, many ingredients ready and I called on Bill to help with the mess of chopping that had to be done. I was putting the bread into the blender to crumb it. There was celery; cranberries, the filbert nuts, onions and I think a few other things all waiting to be chopped by hand. We were working away when a nut would go flying somewhere in the kitchen.

"Keep your hand over them."

"What do you think I'm trying to do?"

Bill sounded frustrated. Then I got hit in the face by a nut.

"Do you want me to do them?" I shouted.

He shouted back, "No I'll do these dam things if it kills me."

As a couple more nuts flew around I heard in a cross voice, "I know why Donald gave you these nuts. He did this once and decided he'd never do it again."

With all the mess around us I had to double up laughing. Bill looked at me and had to laugh himself. We wound up having fun making that stupid stuffing. We both had our hands covered in "gunk" and the phone rang. We looked at each other to see who would answer it, and then I said as I wiped my hands, "I'll get it."

I picked up the phone. It was Rod. He called early in case we'd be out the next day but I told him we were making stuffing for the turkey and told him the mess we were in. "I won't keep you long I just wanted to see how you're doing and wish both of you a Merry Christmas."

"Dad and I were talking about you and Alice and we were thinking it would be nice if next summer we could all arrange to get together at your place on the Cape and have a family reunion. What do you think of that?"

"Well we'll see," he said.

"I don't like we'll see, I like yes."

"But Mom, we just had a family reunion a few months ago in the waiting room of MGH. It's not our fault you weren't there."

I knew then that I must have been getting better. My kids are giving me a hassle again and come to think of it Bill doesn't think I can do no wrong anymore either. I must be a brain tumor survivor, but aren't we all survivors? We drink the wine of life while at the same time we let it sting our lips and burn the cracks. We sing with the birds while we dance on the thorns. We fear the dangers but dare to go forward. We are human and yet we are divine. We fall and rise again to a new beginning, as the phoenix rising from the ashes. We fear one day we may not rise again, but when that day comes, we still survive. Our spirits will look upon those we loved in life and there we will see our faults and our strengths. One is single minded, the other so loving and comforting. There is the thinking one and the joking one, the patient one, the anxious one, but the one quality common to all is the joyfulness and laughter and love shared between them. These gifts live on and our spirit can rest in quiet and tranquility for survival continues.

Three years later

Life was pretty much back to normal. I was getting exercise and feeling pretty good. My balance was never again perfect, nor did I have the energy I used to have but that was a small complaint and may have had something to do with taking so much medication. Our son Rod came by the house with wonderful news. He was being named for a very prestigious award in medical research and we were being invited to the presentation. Within the same week I had to have an MRI and learned that there was a tumor growing on the other side of my brain. After such joyful news, now depressing news. Where do I stand now? I don't know. It will be watched for growth and symptoms. That's all I know.

After getting over the initial shock I decided to just live my life as usual. I did not want anything to spoil the Awards Dinner. I would say nothing about the tumor. I got up one morning and decided to take an early walk as I had often been doing. I walked to a little chapel about a mile away. Out on the lawn there is a statue of the Virgin Mary, with large bushes around, somewhat like a Grotto. I stood before it and looked at the beauty of the sculpture. The facial expression, peaceful yet somber, the hands and fingers so beautifully detailed clasped together as in prayer with the fingers slightly crossed. Then I looked at the feet crushing the head of the serpent. Every detail of the toes is as exquisite as the fingers. I could not but wonder who had created such a beautiful piece. Looking back at the face I thought to myself how privileged Mary was to be chosen to be the one to bear the child Jesus. Then again, how difficult it must have been for her to be betrothed to Joseph and found to be pregnant. At that time a woman could be stoned to death for such a happening. Joy and sorrow mixed again. It has always been and will always be. Life is a succession of Mountains and Valleys. When it is over perhaps we'll see the big picture. If we spend even a little more time on the mountain than we do in the valley, our life will have been a good one. As Kilil Gabran wrote in <u>The</u> <u>Prophet</u>, of joy and sorrow,

> But I say unto you, they are inseparable.

> Together they come, and when one sits alone

> With you at your board,

> Remember that the other is asleep on your bed.

I would like to thank Sally Fairchild, Kay Williamson and Dee Adamcewicz, for the help I received on editing, critiquing and technical assistance.

0-595-22407-5